D0867206

Marketing
and the
bottom line

Reviews of *Marketing and the bottom line*

"This is the era of brands, with a demand-side economy and the increasing value of intangible assets. In this environment, *Marketing and the bottom line* presents a rigorously argued case for measuring the health of business, not only in financial terms but also in the extent to which the business is winning customer preference. Very helpful advice, for chief executives, finance directors and marketing directors, presented in a lively and readable style. A must read for anyone genuinely committed to growing their business organically."

Rupert Howell, President, *Institute of Practitioners in Advertising*

"An excellent book; thoughtful and informative. It will open the minds of board members to the fact that marketing's value can and should, be measured. The data produced is a vital indicator of a company's health."

Mike Mawtus, Vice President, *IBM Euro Global Initiatives*

"I hate this book. It will only encourage the accountants."

Anne Moir, Head of Marketing, *Quadriga Worldwide*

"The book may prove a historic step in putting marketing on every boardroom table. Every director should read it."

David Campbell, Chairman, *The Marketing Society*

"This is a succinct, witty and mould-breaking book on a very important topic. It should be read by all senior managers and marketers."

Professor Hugh Davidson, *Cranfield School of Management*

"This book is a big step forward in assessing marketing impact – an area which is short of regular performance management."

Sir John Egan, Chairman, *MEPC plc*

"This book should be required reading for all board directors. It shows why marketing underpins shareholder value creation, and how marketing effectiveness should be measured and monitored."

Professor Peter Doyle, *Warwick Business School*

"I encourage PLC directors to take a closer look at the sources of cash flow and at marketing as the generator of customer preference. They both need to be regularly measured. This admirable book shows the way."

Sir Michael Perry, CBE, Chairman, *Centrica plc*

In an increasingly competitive world, it is quality
of thinking that gives an edge. An idea that opens new
doors, a technique that solves a problem, or an insight
that simply helps make sense of it all.

We work with leading authors in the fields of
management and finance to bring cutting-edge thinking
and best learning practice to a global market.

Under a range of leading imprints, including
Financial Times Prentice Hall, we create world-class
print publications and electronic products giving readers
knowledge and understanding which can then be
applied, whether studying or at work.

To find out more about our business and professional
products, you can visit us at www.business-minds.com

For other Pearson Education publications, visit
www.pearsoned-ema.com

Marketing
and the
bottom line

The New Metrics of Corporate Wealth

Tim Ambler

An imprint of **Pearson Education**

London · New York · San Francisco · Toronto · Sydney · Tokyo · Singapore
Hong Kong · Cape Town · Madrid · Paris · Milan · Munich · Amsterdam

PEARSON EDUCATION LIMITED

Head Office:
Edinburgh Gate
Harlow CM20 2JE
Tel: +44 (0)1279 623623
Fax: +44 (0)1279 431059

London Office:
128 Long Acre,
London WC2E 9AN
Tel: +44 (0)20 7447 2000
Fax: +44 (0)20 7240 5771
Website: www.business-minds.com

First published in Great Britain in 2000.

© Pearson Education Limited 2000.

The right of Tim Ambler to be identified as Author
of this Work has been asserted by him in accordance
with the Copyright, Designs and Patents Act 1988.

ISBN 0 273 64248 0

British Library Cataloguing in Publication Data
A CIP catalogue record for this book can be obtained from the British Library.

All rights reserved; no part of this publication may be reproduced, stored
in a retrieval system, or transmitted in any form or by any means, electronic,
mechanical, photocopying, recording, or otherwise without either the prior
written permission of the Publishers or a licence permitting restricted copying
in the United Kingdom issued by the Copyright Licensing Agency Ltd,
90 Tottenham Court Road, London W1P 0LP. This book may not be lent,
resold, hired out or otherwise disposed of by way of trade in any form
of binding or cover other than that in which it is published, without the
prior consent of the Publishers.

10 9 8 7 6 5 4 3 2 1

Design by Sue Lamble, Sue Lamble Graphic Design, London.
Typeset by Pantek Arts Ltd, Maidstone, Kent.
Printed and bound in Great Britain by Biddles Ltd, Guildford & King's Lynn.

The Publishers' policy is to use paper manufactured from sustainable forests.

Contents

Acknowledgements   ix

Foreword: Sir Peter Davis   xi

Executive summary   1

Metrics top tables – a summary   14

1 Assessing your present system   17

2 Measuring market-based assets   41

3 Choosing the metrics   57

4 Stages of assessing marketing performance   77

5 Measuring innovation health   95

6 Internal marketing metrics   113

7 Supplying the metrics   131

8 The fuzzy future   146

Appendices

A Assessing advertising and campaigns   154

B Individual metrics   162

C Supplement to innovation health metrics (Chapter 5)   166

117838

Acknowledgements

The sponsors of the Marketing Metrics research project were The Marketing Council, The Marketing Society, the Institute of Practitioners in Advertising, the Sales Promotions Consultants Association and London Business School. The key members of the Steering Group were John Stubbs (TMC), Nick Turnbull and then Mike Detsiny (TMS), Peter Field, Janet Hull and then Hamish Pringle (IPA), Barry Clarke (SPCA) and Professor Patrick Barwise (LBS). Dr Flora Kokkinaki was the key researcher during the first 18 of the 30-month project. Ben Sear (then Diageo), Shashi Halve (British Airways) and Tim Harris undertook key interviewing.

While personal points of view have inevitably crept in, I have attempted to represent the best practitioner-sourced set of UK standards for marketing performance measurement and consistent marketing language. Early and later drafts were critically reviewed by a wide range of senior marketing executives including the Steering Group and James Best, Tim Broadbent, Frank Cokayne, Hugh Davidson, Mike Fisher, Gareth Hill, Nick Kendall, Sarah McMahon, John Mayhead, Peter Mitchell, Raoul Pinnell, Angus Slater, Robin Stotter, Steve Willis and Gerald Wright.

Chapter 2 (brand equity) draws on a joint article with Patrick Barwise, 'The trouble with brand valuation', *Journal of Brand Management*, 5 (5 May), 1998, 367–77. Chapter 6 (internal marketing) draws on work by Kevin Thomson and Lorrie Arganbright. Philip Kleinman, ACNeilsen and Ruth McNeil (Research International) made valuable contributions to Chapter 7 (supplying the metrics). Bettina von Stamm contributed to innovation health metrics and Laura Mazur provided innovation interviews as well as valuable and insightful editing. Also, many thanks to Jo Firth for all her work and support.

Sir Peter Davis found time to contribute a Foreword despite the pressures on his time and of course I will be delighted by any endorsements and post-publication support for this book, which is the culmination of work by so many busy people.

Finally, the FT Prentice Hall team, including Richard Stagg, Jacqueline Cassidy, Lisa Nachtigall, Angela Lewis and Gill Harvey, provided generous and professional help and support. I am immensely grateful.

Foreword

Sir Peter Davis, CEO, Sainsbury plc

Measurement is the company's nervous system. Financial measurements are communicated backwards and forwards, yielding the gross data on a company's wellbeing, the equivalent of pulse, heart rate, calories taken in and spent, in short the evidence of life, and healthy equilibrium. But even our most eminent accountants agree that financial metrics alone can be misleading, and are often incapable of explaining either cause or effect.

Nowadays the unremitting demand for organic growth has led chief executives to turn to the measurement of intangibles for precise evidence of success. Marketing can be described succinctly as 'winning customer preference'. It is critical to competitiveness and wealth creation.

Marketing metrics have the power, as a short scan of the book reveals, to throw light on many of the key questions that beset business leaders. What is our company really worth? Do we have competitive strengths in innovation and branding? Have we achieved sustainable growth based on sound customer strategies?

Too many executive boards have relied too much on the financials. At worst their view of the company can become one-dimensional and *trompe-l'oeil*. If marketing metrics are absent, marketing must admit failure. For without credible metrics, marketing is isolated and such isolation has no place in a modern company.

To promote the measurement of marketing effectiveness both to the profession and to the executive board we first need facts, best practice models and a common language, which we may use to describe and evaluate our marketing assets.

For these reasons The Marketing Council agreed to take a leading role in the work that underpins this book. The project team and Tim Ambler of the London Business School have exceeded expectation and must take credit for promoting the role of science in marketing, and for encouraging the broad uptake of marketing metrics at the level of the executive board. This book represents an advance for marketing and potentially for our national competitiveness.

Executive summary

Any board of directors is naturally preoccupied with its firm's wealth. You would think that it would be equally preoccupied with generating it, but the astonishing fact is that, on average, boards devote nine times more attention to spending and counting cash flow than to wondering where it comes from and how it could be increased.[1] In the monthly accounts, it is common for just one line to be given to the sales revenue from immediate customers. The *source* of the cash flow – the end users – does not even get a mention.[2]

Large companies are understandably concerned with accuracy, but this can lead to endless number crunching. The same profit and loss account numbers are forecasted, then reforecasted, without getting the company any closer to the marketplace. Accountants seem to imagine that a pile of money will grow if only you count it often enough. The point is simple: if you want to know what your future cash flow will look like, investigate where it comes from – the market. A farmer whose livelihood depends on a river flowing through his land will be concerned with the upstream situation, especially if the river could be diverted to a neighbour's property. Yet this is exactly where many boards give too little attention. Our research shows that companies that look to the sources of cash flow – those that think about the market – are more profitable.[3]

Understanding where corporate wealth comes from involves questions like 'Why do *consumers* buy now?', 'Why might they buy more (often)?' and 'Which other kinds of people might buy these products for other reasons?' And in industrial or business-to-business sectors, who *are* the 'consumers' or 'end users'? The train driver has quite different interests from those who buy the trains.

Over the last thirty years, large firms have kept ahead through acquisitions (spending cash again). Even the leading large marketing groups have barely kept up in terms of *organic* growth.[4] In other words, these leaders, such as Unilever, have been paying too little attention to their consumers. They have been looking at the bottom line – net profits or shareholder value – rather than at what generates it. But the game is over: survival depends on basic wealth creation. And wealth creation depends on how healthy the marketing is.

This book summarizes a 30-month research project into 'Marketing Metrics'. Carried out by London Business School, the brief was to report on best practice in marketing performance measurement, to propose improvements and to put forward a shared language. The project sponsors[5] recognized that, unlike accountants, marketers are divided by their understanding of even common words such as 'marketing' or 'brand'. And as well as clarifying the financial aspects of marketing, the project sought to pinpoint the non-financial factors that lead to business success.

This book is not a paean of praise for marketing. What it does is provide guidelines that make marketing fully accountable for the first time. Some marketers may find this greater clarity uncomfortable to live with.

If you think your firm already measures marketing performance adequately, ask yourself these five questions:

1 Do you routinely research consumer behaviour (retention, acquisition, usage etc.) and why consumers behave that way (awareness, satisfaction, perceived quality etc.)?

2 Are the results of this research routinely reported to the board, annually or semi-annually, in a format integrated with financial marketing metrics?

3 In those reports, are the results compared with the levels previously forecasted in the business plans?

4 Are they also compared with the levels achieved by your key competitor using the same indicators?

5 Is short-term performance adjusted according to the change in your market-based asset(s)?

If the answer to any of those questions is 'no', then your system is not good enough. Read on. This is a brief summary of what comes next. We look at how market health leads to corporate wealth, by considering:

- The reasons for regular marketing assessment by the whole board;

- The key marketplace metrics. We are looking for indicators of the health of the sources of cash flow;

- Innovation health;

- Employee metrics. End users are the ultimate customers, but your own staff are your first. You need to measure the health of the internal market;

- Getting and managing marketing information;

- Action this day: five recommendations for immediate implementation.

Before we plunge in, however, we need to clarify language.

Language

Tedious though it may seem, we must define 'marketing', 'brand', 'brand equity' and 'metrics'. Too many companies dismiss the importance of marketing merely because they do not understand what it is. Take the Confederation of British Industry, for example. In their new Fit for the Future campaign,[6] innovation and competitiveness are rightly extolled, but marketing and customers of any kind barely get a mention. Alec Daly, the Campaign Chairman, says, 'We want companies who find it difficult to innovate talking to those where innovation is inbred; companies who find it difficult to control cash, talking to those who find it second nature; and companies who need and want a step change in their competitive performance, exposed to those who have already done it.' This is all admirable, but it is also production-oriented, and ignores the outside world – the market.

When people say 'marketing', they may mean any one of three things: 'pan-company', 'functional' or 'budgetary' marketing. The first, perhaps ugly, expression describes a holistic view of marketing: it is what the whole company does, not just the 'marketers', to secure customer preference and thereby achieve higher returns for the shareholder. Bass, the beer and leisure group, now sees marketing in these terms; and according to the publishing company EMAP, 'Marketing is central to our business here. This is a total marketing company and everyone is interested in marketing'.[7] Consciously or not, every company in the world engages in marketing in this primary sense. Pan-company marketing is therefore not an option but a necessity: you engage in it whether you like it or not. The difference is between those who consciously espouse this customer-oriented philosophy and those who market by happenstance.

'Functional' marketing is what marketing professionals do, and this varies from company to company. It often implies that marketing is restricted to the activities of one department, but this isn't necessarily the case. Few small companies have marketing departments and even large firms, like the Unilever beauty products subsidiary Elida Gibbs, are dispersing their marketers throughout the organization. In terms of responsibility, some marketers are not accountable for profits whereas others see this as their main charge. Some have charge of product specification, pricing, sales and trade marketing functions whereas others are seen as staffers, outside the main direction of the business.

The third definition of marketing, in terms of 'budgetary expenditure', refers largely to advertising and promotion. When people talk of the 'return' on marketing, this is the marketing they generally mean. But the incremental gain on the advertising and promotional expenditures should be evaluated in the context of the wider meanings of marketing. Guidelines for assessing advertising and promotional performance form Appendix A.

The first definition of marketing is the most important. Only a minority of companies have separate marketing departments, or separate marketing budgets, but they all have end users to satisfy. We shall address the secondary meanings, but we are going to focus on maximizing marketing health throughout the *whole* company's business in order to maximize corporate wealth. By the end of the book, pan-company marketing will have been extended to include employees (the 'employer brand' and the internal market) and all forms of innovation that affect the market. But we can leave those extensions for later.

'**Brand**', once used only for consumer goods, is a term that now appears in every sector. For example, Compass, the business-to-business catering firm, is a brand and so is the Church of England. While the word began as simply an identifying symbol, today it includes the whole bundle of benefits for the end user. Most, but not all, UK marketers now mean:

Brand = Product + Packaging + Added values

In the case of industrial, service or retail marketing, the packaging is not, of course, a physical wrapping, but whatever way the product is presented: a retail shop front, for example. The added values are the ways that the consumer thinks about the product, for example as 'cheap and cheerful', innovative, only for kids, and so on. They may be psychological – the *perceived* quality and economic benefits, over and above those provided by the product itself.[8]

Industrial and business-to-business marketers tend not to use the word 'brand' and attribute added values, if they think about them at all, to reputation or goodwill. Of course people are entitled to use whatever language suits them, but to achieve cross-sector common language for this book, a 'brand' is what every added-value business sells, irrespective of sector.

Good marketing builds the firm's intangible assets. We need a single term to describe it, whatever the sector. Metrics research has shown that 'brand equity' is by far the most frequent term for this asset and it is adopted here. Marketing can be seen as building brand equity: if a company gets that right, profits will largely take care of themselves. In British Airways, for instance, the key corporate asset is called the 'Masterbrand' and understanding this brand equity is a key marketing responsibility.

Brand equity is often equated with **brand valuation** but that is like confusing your house (asset) with its financial worth (price). You cannot live in a price ticket. Brand equity is the whole asset built by marketing and exists largely in the heads of stakeholders of all kinds, but most importantly in those of the end users. The brand equity in the distribution channels and in the minds of employees matters too. The valuation (or value) is what the asset is worth.

To stay with our original farmer metaphor, brand equity is the upstream dam that stores the water for when it is needed. The dam is topped up in the good times and is not allowed to drain too far down in the bad. Advertising tops it up. Perhaps the dam should be seen as supplying both the water and the power for the farm. Nothing is more crucial to business success.

Back in the 1980s, no firms were formally measuring brand equity. By 2010, no professionally managed business will fail to do so.

Finally, a 'metric' is a performance measure that top management should review. It is a measure that matters to the whole business. The term comes from music and implies regularity: the reviews should typically take place yearly or half-yearly. Pepsico, for example, uses a full year's data every six months and considers more frequent *complete* reviews unhelpful. Obviously some metrics, like sales, are reviewed monthly. Metrics is not just another word for measure: metrics should be necessary (i.e. the company cannot do without them), precise, consistent and sufficient (i.e. comprehensive) for review purposes.

Metrics may be financial (usually from the profit and loss account), from the marketplace, or from non-financial internal sources (innovation and employee). **'Diagnostics'** are lower-level measures that explain variances, e.g. sales by channel. **'Derivatives'** are trends, e.g. sales this year as a percent of last year's. '**Double derivatives**' show the rate of change in the trend, e.g. whether the rate of sales increase is slowing down.

So much for language. Now we can continue.

Reasons for regular marketing assessment by the board

Companies cannot survive without marketing, though they may call it something different or not even notice that they are doing it. Securing customer preference opens up the main cash flow for every business. Here are five reasons why *all* boards should give priority to marketing metrics:

- Marketing is *how* the firm secures its key objectives, i.e. it sources the cash flow. On the widely accepted basis that a firm is more likely to achieve what it measures, any board should review those indicators it considers to be the most significant milestones along its intended path, i.e. the metrics.

- They discourage *short termism*. Some top executives, including Lord Sheppard, then Chairman of the GrandMet alcoholic beverages, Pillsbury and Burger King company, used to dismiss the need for balancing short- and long-term priorities on the grounds that the long term is merely the sum of all the short terms. Optimizing the short term, in his view, took care of the long. That is only true if brand equity, the brand's health in its internal and external markets, is adjusted for. If the asset has grown, the short-term profits are enhanced, but if it has weakened, the short-term profits are misleadingly high. Marketing metrics provide the diagnosis.

- *Marketers should be accountable.* John Hooper, Director General of the Incorporated Society of British Advertisers, recently said, 'Everyone accepts that measuring the performance of marketing communications programmes is vitally important, but the reality today is that this issue does not feature in most marketing directors' top ten priorities.'[9] Few firms today pay their advertising or promotions agencies by results. Why ever not? In future this will become common practice. Procter and Gamble set the lead in October 1999.

- As noted above, *market-oriented, customer-focused companies are more profitable* than those primarily concerned with production, the bottom line or other stakeholders. And market-oriented companies can be identified by the attention they give to marketing metrics.[10]

- *Metrics are essential for debriefing.* Firms devote far more resources to planning, which may just reinforce behaviour, than they do to debriefing, which may change it. US fighter pilots, for example, are trained more in the debriefing than in the preparation or in the flying. Debriefing is frank and can be painful but it is where behaviour is changed. Interestingly, rank is no protection. A colonel is unlikely to fly missions very often. So when they do, they are treated as rookie pilots and debriefed accordingly. What matters is that the next mission learns from the one before.

Key marketplace metrics

To be realistic about short-term performance, we need to adjust for changes in the marketing asset from the beginning to the end of the period, usually the financial year. This is no different from the treatment of any other assets – the inventory, for example. Unless we do this we cannot know if the short term is just living off the accumulated but unrealized assets of the past or whether it is building assets for the future. Is the cash flow in the upstream dam increasing or reducing?

Marketing performance evaluation splits into two parts: the short-term results and the adjustment for the change in brand equity. The short term is usually provided by the profit and loss (P&L) account, though firms differ on whether to focus on the top line (sales turnover), the bottom (shareholder value), somewhere in between, or some combination of all these.

The financial results are driven by sales turnover (trade customer) less (marketing) costs. The other key metrics summarized in Figure 1 are non-financial: consumer intermediate (what is in the consumer's head) and consumer behaviour, which is always driven by the brain, however unconsciously. Both of these categories of metric can be compared with competitor performance. Marketing, and that includes innovation as discussed in the next section, interacts both with direct customers, via employees, and consumers, via advertising and promotion.

Our research showed that metrics fell into categories that are determined by the nature of the business. For example, at Cadbury, the confectionery company, key measures include performance against strategic milestones, market share, advertising spend, brand and advertising awareness, penetration and average weight of purchase and percentage of total volume accounted for by new products. At retail bank Lloyds/TSB, key metrics are the numbers of new customers gained and retained.

Retail chains, such as McDonald's, substitute the retail branch for the trade customer and monitor both branches (e.g. using mystery shoppers[11]) and consumers. For McDonald's, brand equity has become increasingly important since they introduced the concept in the early 1990s.

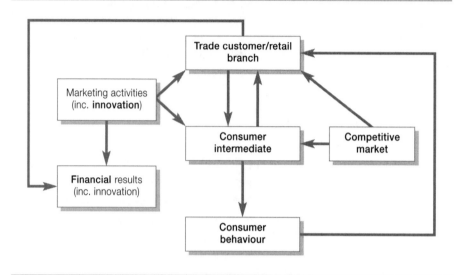

Fig 1 ■ Metrics categories

Metrics have simply evolved from custom and practice, not scientific analysis. We found the UK top ten brand equity metrics in terms of company usage to be as shown in Table 1.

Table 1 ■ Most commonly used metrics

Metric	% of firms using measure	% that reach the top board	% giving top rating for assessing marketing performance
Awareness	78.0	28.0	28.0
Market share (volume or value)	78.0	33.5	36.5
Relative price (market share value/volume)	70.0	34.5	37.5
Number of complaints (level of dissatisfaction)	69.0	30.0	45.0
Consumer satisfaction	68.0	36.0	46.5
Distribution/availability	66.0	11.5	18.0
Total number of customers	65.5	37.4	40.0
Perceived quality/esteem	64.0	32.0	35.5
Loyalty/retention	64.0	50.7	67.0
Relative perceived quality	62.5	52.8	61.6

The second and third columns of figures in this table show the percentage that reach the top board and their importance for marketing performance assessment. These move reasonably in step, as they should, but note the low ratings for usefulness given to awareness and distribution. The data was collected from 200 top marketers and finance executives. Appendix B expands on the most-used marketing metrics.

These metrics are calculated differently in different sectors. For example, loyalty may be the share of category requirements in packaged goods markets, e.g. the amount of Persil a user buys as a percentage of total laundry detergent purchases, or the churn rate (brand to brand conversions) in communications businesses such as Vodafone.

So far we have focused on customers at various levels through to the ultimate users. For many metrics the question is not how satisfied the customer is, but how this compares with how satisfied the competitors' customers are. They may be the same people. An 80% satisfaction level is great if it is 70% for the competition, but not so good if theirs is 90%. Similarly, no board should ignore the *relative* prices of their main products, nor their consumers' perceptions *relative* to the way their competitors are seen. About two-thirds of our respondent firms seem not to review these data at board level.

Before tackling the difficult question of how a firm should decide which metrics matter most for them, we need to take a look at innovation and employees.

Innovation health

Our research found general and increasing recognition of the importance of innovation. Top managements want to monitor 'innovativeness' and yet few believe that key performance indicators (KPIs) provide the solution. Boots the Chemist, the UK's major health and beauty care retailer, has appointed a director of innovation, but carries out little measurement beyond the number of product launches and the proportion of sales from recent launches.

The crux is the *quality* of innovation, not the quantity. Indeed, many large firms today suffer from an excess of innovation, or initiative overload. The three phases of innovation (creativity, development and implementation) require different skills. Culture (the way things are done) and process (what is done) are merely enablers, not drivers.

3M very successfully uses just a few simple metrics, such as the proportion of sales due to recent innovations. Many other firms have copied these metrics, but few have succeeded because their leadership styles and cultures are different. The moral is that firms should get away from the detail and first measure these bigger-picture variables.

Thus it is mostly a question of leadership, and then culture, rather than process. In large companies, much of the process gets in the way and should be dismantled. These metrics are very similar to those used for assessing employer brand equity, i.e. what the employees carry around in their heads about the firm they work for. J A Sharwood, for example, markets a range of ethnic chutneys and sauces. It has found that complex mission and value statements, and detailed objectives, are too difficult to communicate and so the company is constantly seeking ways of simplification.

Employee metrics

Some companies, and especially consumer service companies, see employees as their first customers. If management correctly markets to employees, then the front line employees will take care of the external customers. In this perception, internal marketing becomes, for the board, more important than external marketing and needs its own set of metrics. Whether 'marketing' includes employees is academic: synergizing human resource and marketing skills can bring rich rewards. The 'employer brand' concept helps these two functions to learn from each other. Tobacco company Gallaher, for example, sees marketing in pan-company terms and has marketing, sales and financial people working together in teams.

There is no need to debate which segment of 'customer' is the most important. Just as a sequence of events, employee issues will need to be addressed first and the end user will be satisfied last. Marketers will *plan* things the other way about, i.e. start with the consumer, but the motivation of all the segments needs to be measured whichever way the company goes.

Many firms now measure employee indicators but few cross-fertilize employee and customer survey techniques and measures. They should; the relationship between employee and customer satisfaction is commonplace.[12] BP Amoco found, unsurprisingly, a good correlation between the two. To some extent, employees can provide, far more cheaply and easily, proxies for external research though this needs careful quality control. In a service company especially, customers form their impressions, i.e. brand equity, from their interactions with the employees.

Getting and managing marketing information

Marketing metrics are difficult to assemble. Different measures are scattered all over large companies for different time periods, different customer and stakeholder segments, and a multitude of purposes. Each market research firm supplies data efficiently, according to its own system. This keeps costs down and makes the information affordable, but it does not make it comparable. It may be easier to commission new research than to locate reports that are gathering dust.

This is not about fiddling with costs but taking a holistic approach to external and internal marketing information: the information is mostly there, but someone needs to take charge of bringing it all together.

Very large companies may, like Unilever, have scope for a department that specializes in marketing information, independent from their marketers. But for most companies, the only function in a position to integrate financial and non-financial marketing metrics is the finance department. In other words, you should **turn over market research responsibility to the finance director or chief knowledge officer.**

This proposal is clearly contentious, but here are some reasons why it deserves serious consideration:

- Marketers are widely seen as selective and/or manipulative in the way they present information. Independence would add credibility.

- As John Hooper says, metrics are not high on marketers' priorities. Most managers are fed up with surveys and questions from business schools. Even so, we were surprised by the low interest shown by marketers. With honourable exceptions (notably those who contributed to this book), marketers are more interested in making runs than scoring. Perhaps this is as it should be.

- Marketing information is widely dispersed in large organizations. Only part of it exists in the marketing department, even if there is one.

Action this day

Understanding and nurturing the sources of cash flow deserves a prime position on every board agenda and substantial attention every six months at least. Making the space, and hoping the marketers will fill it, is not enough. It is an old joke, but marketing really is too important to be left to marketers.

Can the needs identified here be met by a few simple metrics that every firm can use? The idea of having a general, universal approach is beguiling and has been a constant challenge throughout this research project. But the short answer is 'no'. Marketing metrics are marker posts along the company's chosen strategic route. To suggest all companies should have the same, and only the same, metrics is to suggest that all companies should have the same marketing strategy. Since differentiation lies at the heart of marketing, such an outcome would guarantee failure for them all. Metrics should be tailored to the company's strategy, although some metrics, e.g. market share, should certainly be general and thus comparable.

Boards should be wary of calls for oversimplification. We are not dealing with a hygiene matter where boxes can quickly be ticked before moving on. Indeed, using marketing metrics in a mechanistic way denies their very purpose. Even if the metrics are the same, the sources of cash flow – the reasons why consumers buy and might buy more – are the discussions the metrics should trigger. The book offers a design process to decide the right marketing metrics for your company, taking both the tailored and general points of view into account.

Here is a crucial point: there are no measures of corporate health but only of ill health. If there is nothing wrong with you after a battery of tests, then you are well. That is why firms need multiple measures and why the measures need to be relevant to the company's situation. Few men need pregnancy testing and few business-to-business companies have to worry about share of (advertising) voice. What matters is for each firm to determine the relevant-to-them indicators of internal and external market health – or ill health, as the case may be.

Here are five things the board needs to put into action, and today is as good a time as any:

- Appoint a team, led by a board member, ideally the chief executive, to develop the metrics reporting system. This should be aligned with customer insights, business strategy, goals and required performance. Include marketing information responsibilities in their terms of reference.

- Ensure it is cross-disciplinary with members from finance, human resources, sales and marketing (at least).

- Give them a six-month deadline, with an interim board report after three.

- Publicize the task and the reasons for it, and encourage worldwide participation. Set out the new language of measurement, the intention to compare financial and market measures against both plan and external benchmarks and the role of brand equity. Constructive participation requires the ground rules to be made explicit.

■ When the selection of metrics is at an advanced stage, the board should participate in the final inclusion/exclusion decisions. Put the meeting on the calendar now.

Just as gold prospectors celebrated when they departed for the hills, so any company should rejoice when it sets out to rediscover the sources of its cash flow. A healthy flow will provide the wealth for everything else.

References

1 Marketing Metrics project research with UK PLCs, December 1999.

2 Operational matters, supplies and suppliers, corporate governance, employee issues, interest, taxes, dividends, and capital expenditure take far more time than the motivations of the ultimate customer. But these are all ways to spend, or at least count, the cash, not increase its flow.

3 We found a 0.25 correlation between customer orientation and performance. The precise figures vary but this result is similar to comparable studies noted in the book.

4 David Cowans' Marketing Forum Presentation, *Oriana*, September 1999.

5 See acknowledgements.

6 Website: www.fitforthefuture.org.uk

7 Quoted in 'The Role of Marketing', research report by KPMG, 1999, 7.

8 The formal attribution of added values to the three types still taught today goes back to a follower of St Thomas Aquinas. San Bernadino of Siena (1380–1444) distinguished between *virtuositas* (function), *raritas* (scarcity or market price) and *complacibilitas* (psychological benefits). Merchants were entitled to take all three into account in determining the *justum pretium* (just price) of goods. Source: Blaug, Mark (ed.) (1991) *St Thomas Aquinas (1225–1274)*, Aldershot: Edward Elgar Publishing.

9 John Hooper, CBE, Director General, Incorporated Society of British Advertisers, 21 October 1999.

10 Data from the Marketing Metrics research project.

11 Market researchers who visit as surrogate shoppers or diners and report back on their experiences.

12 This is developed in Chapter 6 with citations.

Metrics top tables

Standard P&L metrics

Actual metric	% compared with plan	% compared with competition	. Board review frequency
Sales	Volume/value	Market share	Monthly
Marketing investment	Period costs	Share of voice	Quarterly
Bottom line	e.g. profit	Share of profit	Half-yearly*

* **1** The board will review the company's sales and bottom line, certainly monthly and maybe weekly, but this is the profit by brand market unit (BMU) analysis.

   2 First and second order derivatives (trends and rates of change in trends) are more important for board review than snapshot metrics.

   3 The availability of diagnostics for analyzing variances in metrics is assumed.

General brand equity metrics

Consumer metric	Measured by
Relative satisfaction	Consumer preference or satisfaction as per cent average for market/competitor(s). The competitive benchmark should be stated
Commitment	Index of switchability (or some similar measure of retention, loyalty, purchase intent, or bonding)
Relative perceived quality	Perceived quality satisfaction as per cent average for market/competitor(s). The competitive benchmark should be stated
Relative price	Market share (value)/Market share (volume)
Availability	Distribution, e.g. weighted per cent of retail outlets carrying the brand

Innovation metrics short list (Chapter 5)

Strategy	Awareness of goals (vision)
	Commitment to goals (vision)
	Active innovation support
	Resource adequacy
Culture	Appetite for learning
	Freedom to fail
Outcomes	No. of initiatives in process
	No. of innovations launched
	% of revenue due to launches during last 3 years

Employee metrics (Chapter 6)

Awareness of goals

Commitment to goals

Appetite for learning

Freedom to fail

Relative employee satisfaction

Aggregate customer brand empathy
(Composite index of how well employees see company brands as consumers do)

1

Assessing your present system

The Executive Summary showed why every firm should regularly assess marketing performance. So what happens next? While no two firms address the question in quite the same way, this chapter provides the cross-range of answers that you need.

Figure 1.1 gives an overview:

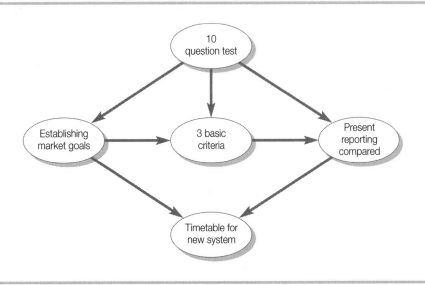

Fig 1.1 ■ How well do we assess external and internal market health now?

In our research, we found that most firms don't have a clear picture of their overall marketing performance. They prefer to fumble around in the dark. It's easy to see why: fumbling has a lot going for it. More adventure, more creativity, more surprises and more fantasies are all possible. But you may not like what you see when the lights do go on. Clarity of goals and metrics separates the professional from the amateur. To be a professional marketer, you should be quantifying what you do to make sure that it is constantly improving.

Top athletes also use measurement to motivate themselves to higher levels of performance. This isn't to say you should be adopting petty rules and standards, but you should be looking for new and different ways of driving yourself forward. In the final chapter we will address the dangers of giving metrics excessive importance, but first we need to recognize how powerful these tools can be.

Table 1.1 provides a test for your firm's marketing performance assessment system. Complete the test for the fun of it. You will find the scores in the references for this chapter.[1] The total score is not as important as coming to terms with the issues.

Remember, taking marketing on board is the crucial first stage. Everything else is relatively straightforward.

This chapter covers the following key points:

■ What marketing means in practice. We take a closer look at how marketing generates cash flow.

■ Top-down marketing assessment. Advertising and promotion should only be evaluated in the context of overall marketing performance.

■ The three basic criteria for marketing assessment: subjectivity (assessing performance against internal plans), objectivity (against the market or competitors), and adjustment for brand equity.

■ The challenge of more complex brand architectures. Large companies have many brands in many markets, so providing the board with details of all these would be excessive. Multinationals select those that matter most.

■ Sector issues. Metrics considerations across business sectors are more alike than different, but these differences need attention.

■ Will you need a task force? The diversity of marketing metrics sources and the entrenched nature of existing systems make it highly likely that any large company will need a powerful task force to effect change.

Table 1.1 ■ Ten questions to rate your firm's marketing assessment system

1 Does the board regularly and formally assess marketing performance?
   (a) Yearly (b) Six-monthly (c) Quarterly (d) More often (e) Rarely (f) Never

2 Does it distinguish the three meanings of 'marketing'?
   (a) Yes, all three (b) Well, two anyway (c) No

3 Does the firm have business/marketing plans?
   (a) Yes, formal (b) Yes, informal (c) No

4 Does the business/marketing plan show the *non-financial* corporate goals and link them to market goals?
   (a) No/no plan (b) Corporate no, market yes (c) Yes to both

5 Does the plan show the comparison of your marketing performance with competitors or the market as a whole?
   (a) No/no plan (b) Yes, clearly (c) In between

6 What is your main marketing asset called?
   (a) Brand equity (b) Reputation (c) Other term (d) We have no term

7 Does the review involve internal (e.g. plan) and external (e.g. competitive) benchmarks adjusted for changes in the marketing assets?
   (a) Yes (b) No (c) Partially

8 Do you review the contribution of functional marketing, and then budgets, on a top-down basis to isolate return on marketing investment (ROI)?
   (a) No (b) Functional and budget together (c) Functional and then budget

9 How aligned are the performance *measures*? Are all the external and internal indicators for identical markets, segments, time periods etc.?
   (a) Not at all (b) Somewhat (c) Quite well

10 (Skip this if your firm is single-brand and single-market)
   How confident are you in matching marketing inputs and outputs, e.g. by using a BMU system?
   (a) Our system is fine (b) So so (c) We really cannot be sure of market performance contributions except for the group as a whole

What marketing means in practice

Marketing is the means whereby a firm achieves its key objectives. This bold claim turns on the 'pan-company' definition of marketing, which is what the **whole company** does to secure customer preference and thereby achieve higher returns for the shareholder. Seeing things entirely from the customer's side makes no more sense than taking a uniquely shareholder viewpoint: the art lies in using consumer empathy to achieve wins for both sides.

The market-oriented firm *consciously* takes the consumer's viewpoint first. Other orientations regard customers, if they regard them at all, as somewhere between an important means of satisfying shareholders and a necessary nuisance. More likely, they have simply delegated thinking about them to the sales force.

Professionalism means moving market orientation up from being an unconscious, instinctive philosophy to purposefully and consistently walking the consumer talk. This is best expressed by measuring key end user and competitor attitudes and behaviour.

So from here on, 'pan-company marketing' refers to a market-oriented firm consciously and consistently putting customers (end users) first, in order to understand and meet their needs better – better than before and better than competitors. Research shows that these are also the firms that make more money than their otherwise-oriented cousins.[2] Yet these other orientations are deeply rooted. Ever since Ricardo vanquished Malthus in their supply versus demand debates of 200 years ago, supply-side thinking has dominated British business. The 'supply chain', for example, should be considered from the other end and termed the 'demand chain'.

The board needs to begin with the wider perception of marketing and only then should it consider whether specialist marketers, and budgets, are needed. Most small companies do not need a specialist department. Advertising, promotions and other specialist marketing activities may just appear in the general budget. On the other hand, all firms need a consumer-first attitude. Different firms assign these responsibilities in different ways. While British Airways, for example, regards marketing as extremely important, the specialist marketers do not have direct responsibility for all four Ps (product, price, promotion and place, i.e. distribution) of marketing.

British Airways

In British Airways (BA), marketing is a functional department; distribution and pricing are non-marketing responsibilities. The total airline performance is formally reviewed both monthly and annually with the key methods of measurement being the results of various awareness and customer satisfaction monitors, customer relations feedback, market share data etc. The monitors now used are a relatively new set and have evolved over the

Marketing
and the
bottom line

FINANCIAL TIMES
Prentice Hall

A recommended approach to measuring brand equity[12]

The difficulty with brand equity is that it cannot be measured directly. We cannot look inside people's heads and count the brand synapses (memories), nor can we quantify brand bytes in computer programs and business systems. So we have to use proxies of three kinds: inputs, intermediate measures and behaviour. Figure 2.5 gives an overview of consumer brand equity. Competitor effects are not shown but should be noted. The score relative to competition is generally a better indicator than any score for the brand in isolation.

■ *Inputs* include the amount of advertising and communications (the prime driver of brand equity).

■ *Intermediate measures* seek to estimate what is in people's heads directly. Awareness and attitudes such as how relevant they perceive the brand to be to them, its perceived quality and customer satisfaction provide fuzzy data needing care in interpretation even if collected to the highest standards. Such responses are unreliable, especially emotions and feelings. We are good at answering questions about what we *have done* and what we *know*, but neuroscience indicates caution about reported feelings and intentions.

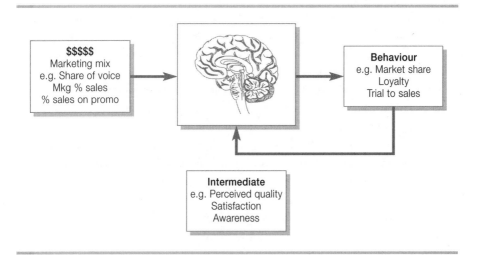

Fig 2.5 ■ **Measures of consumer brand equity***· These measures may be absolute or relative to competition

■ *Behaviour* is widely considered to be the most reliable indicator of what we really think and feel. Sales are the most popular metric. Perhaps the next most useful are market share and relative price (share of market by value divided by share of market by volume), provided that it is sustainable in terms of quality and reputation. Customer gains, retention, loyalty, penetration and whether the brand appeals to frequent or occasional users are also popular.

All these metrics can be *absolute* (sales or awareness) or *relative*, like market share and relative price, which are expressed as ratios to the market as a whole or to major competitors. As noted above, the relative measures are generally more useful. For example, the *absolute* level of customer satisfaction has been shown to be an unreliable indicator whereas satisfaction *relative* to the target competitor is a better predictor of performance. That makes sense: however good you may be, you still have to be better than your competitors. Even that may not be enough. Good performance measurement requires *both* competitive *and* absolute measures to be compared to plan targets.

Marketing, then, is first and foremost the building of brand equity. Do that right and profits will take care of themselves. Brand equity is not something apart from but central to business decision-making.

Measurement has two primary roles: control and direction. Marketers recognize the importance of control but dislike the inhibition. This colours all assessment metrics, which is a pity. Audacious targets, well presented, can be motivational and even inspirational. Top board metrics flag what directors really care about because management's orientation is apparent from the numbers they ask to see. *Nothing better demonstrates the market orientation of a business than the board requiring regular measures of brand equity.* And that is a flag that marketers can salute.

Measuring brand equity and performance also gives marketing, finance and other managers a shared language to debate their brands' strategies and positioning, together with the drivers of success in the market.

In larger firms with formal systems, brand equity measurement frequency is set by the planning and reporting cycle. Since brand equity should be an intrinsic component of performance review and decision-making, the more cycles there are, the greater the frequency. Major decisions to cut or increase marketing functions and/or expenditure are often taken mid-year in response to changing circumstances. The basic principle is that marketing decisions should be based on brand equity as well as profit considerations.

Small and medium-sized firms, however, may not have formal planning systems at all. In this case, an annual review of marketing performance and brand equity may well be enough. No firm is too small for the questions 'What are we trying to do?', 'Compared to that, how *are* we doing?' and 'In the light of that, what *should* we be doing?'

Marketing performance, in essence, is given by short-term results adjusted by the gain or decrease in the marketing asset. No one can measure the future. Brand equity – or whatever term is used for the marketing asset – stands for the present value of future performance *in so far as it has already been earned.* We should not take into account the future results from future activities. This concept of assets as representing stores of future value is nothing new. 'Debtors', in the balance sheet, stands for money that will be paid and 'stocks' for goods that will be sold. Brand equity may not feature on the balance sheet but it is an asset in exactly that sense: it is the storehouse of *future* profits that result from *past* marketing activities.

Executive minutes 2

1 Board to determine clear use of marketing language, including brand equity and valuation, metrics and diagnostics. Consider defining brand equity as 'what is in people's heads about the brand'.

2 Board to ensure its chosen framework for brand equity metrics and its reporting timetable are considered by the marketing metrics task force.

3 Finance director to report on relative importance of brand equity/equities compared to other company assets and brand equity measurement strategy.

4 Board to be informed annually about brand equity for each 'customer' segment (consumers/end users, direct trade customers, employees, shareholders etc.) by the relevant functional director (marketing, sales, human resources, investor relations etc.).

5 Finance director to provide annual valuations of the (leading) brand(s) within the total brand equity measurement system.

6 Brand equity to be considered alongside profitability for all major business decisions.

References

1 Ehrenberg, Andrew S.C. (1994) 'The case against brand equity: if you're strong why aren't you bigger?', *Admap* (October), 13–14.

2 Aaker, David A. (1991) *Managing Brand Equity*, New York: Free Press. See also (1996) *Building Strong Brands*, New York: Free Press.

3 Srivastava, Rajendra K. and Shocker, Allan D. (1991) 'Brand equity: a perspective on its meaning and measurement', Cambridge, Mass.: Marketing Science Institute, working paper #91–124.

4 Keller, Kevin L. (1998) *Strategic Brand Management*, Upper Saddle River, NJ: Prentice Hall.

5 Shaw, Robert (1998) *Improving Marketing Effectiveness*, London: Economist Books.

6 Barwise, Patrick. (1993) 'Brand equity: Snark or Boojum?', *International Journal of Marketing Research* 10 (1 March), 93–104.

7 Carsberg, Sir Bryan (1998) 'Future directions of financial reporting', in Carey, Anthony and Sancto, Juliana (eds.), *Performance Measurement in the Digital Age*, London: Institute of Chartered Accountants of England and Wales, 36–40.

8 Hall and Partners (1999) *A Brief Word About Us*, London.

9 Richmond Events (1995, 1996, 1997) research reports from the *Canberra* (27–30 September), *Oriana* (25–28 September) and *Oriana* (17–20 September), Richmond, Surrey.

10 Davis, Scott and Douglass, Darrell. (1995) 'Holistic approach to brand equity management', *Marketing News* (16 January), 4–5.

11 The Marketing Council booklet (1999) 'The whole company ... designed for customers'.

12 This section is based on best current practice established during the Marketing Metrics research project.

3

Choosing the metrics

No market research agency will provide your company with a complete ready-packaged set of metrics, and few companies design a set of metrics from scratch: they begin with what they already have and proceed incrementally. It is very unlikely, therefore, that we shall find any single pattern, or discover one that could, or should, be enforced. Selecting which metrics to recommend prompted two quite different pieces of advice from senior directors in leading companies. We may have to choose between these competing approaches – the general and the tailored:

■ 'Keep your metrics down to the few which can be applied in every company. Don't complicate it with long lists or advise every company to choose a different set. The metrics message will not get across unless it is simple and, to make comparisons, everyone needs to be doing the same. Companies should be required to report these few universals externally as well as using them internally.'

■ 'No two companies are alike. Strategically they should start with their own objectives. The brand's positioning should decide the metrics but as positioning requires differentiation, metrics will differ. Only when they know exactly what they are trying to achieve can they choose the measures that matter.'

Figure 3.1 provides an overview of this chapter. First we need to define the brand, the market and the customer segment for which we are determining the metrics. Then we explore both paths: the general approach described above, which leads us to three profit and loss account and five

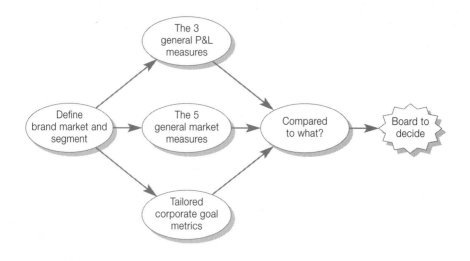

Fig 3.1 ■ Choosing the metrics

brand equity metrics; and the tailored approach, which can be adopted in place of the general or in addition to it.

Note that we are still considering overall marketing performance. Appendix A deals with assessing the performance of advertising and promotional campaigns, including the tricky issue of what costs should be charged to marketing. (If it is intended to build brand equity, go ahead and charge it to marketing. Otherwise do not.)

Both the metrics and the process of choosing them are illustrative. Firms need to work their own way through the minefield that is metrics, precisely because metrics are in themselves signposts towards the firm's unique goals.

Most systems will have a mix of the two approaches. They are separated here for exposition.

The general approach: Below board level, large firms have so many market measures that they find it hard to choose between them. The best generally applicable set of metrics probably involves comparing three basic profit and loss account metrics (sales, marketing spend and profit) against plan and competition.

The change of the marketing asset, or brand equity, needs five indicators, such as market share, to be compared from the start to the end of the period in question. Universality is only conceptual: the *way* the figures are calculated will still depend on sector and relevance. For example, customer loyalty might be measured by retention in one kind of business and the share of category requirements, e.g. how many times a user buys Persil out of their total purchases of laundry detergents, in another.

The tailored approach: Either this requires an explicit definition of your firm's strategic objectives or, less good but more practical for some, they can be deduced from the metrics the board wants to see. Changing objectives from year to year plays havoc with consistent measurement systems, and benchmarking moving competitors is even more difficult.

Gallaher, one of the most professional marketing companies, uses a broad set of financial and non-financial market indicators, but the emphasis is on comparison with the competition.

Gallaher

Nigel Northridge is Marketing and Sales Director for the UK company. Marketing performance is reviewed at every executive meeting on their general principle of 'justify or eliminate'. Financial measures are the most important, followed by competitive, consumer and then innovation. The company sees itself as competitively oriented and uses war games to review competitor strategies.

Marketing is understood in the pan-company sense. One recent change is to make the agency the brand custodian, i.e. not just responsible for advertising. Another is to increase inter-functional teamwork with more brand, as distinct from activity, orientation. Marketers are increasing their financial literacy. Northridge sees Gallaher as being at the 'many' stage of metrics evolution.

Source: Metrics interview with Nigel Northridge, Marketing and Sales Director, 14 October 1998.

Defining the brand market segment

There are a number of points to bear in mind. First, the unit for marketing assessment in this chapter is a single brand market segment – in other words, one brand's performance in one marketplace in relation to just one consumer segment. More complex organizations, which have many brands in many markets, each selling to distinct segments, need to deconstruct the business into these units for marketing assessment purposes. The assumption is that there are trade customers and competition as well as a single end user segment. Not a very heavy assumption since, for chain retailing, branch managers and franchisees take the place of trade customers. This structure applies equally to industrial and business-to-business marketing where the buyers and the operators (end users) are different people.

Figure 3.2 shows, quite simply, the sales from the company and the competition to trade customers and onward to end users. If measuring marketing performance was just a matter of sales, we could stop there. Note that this model continues to omit environmental factors for the reasons described in Chapter 1, viz. they are outside the marketers' control.

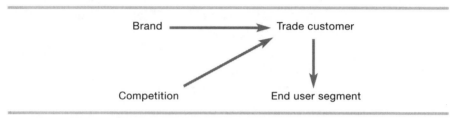

Fig 3.2 ■ Brand market segment

For marketers, defining the 'market' is an art form. J&B Rare had annually increasing market shares in the US in the 1980s despite falling sales in a static market. Was that possible? The local marketing team redefined their market, first to Scotch imported in bottle, and then to premium Scotch imported in bottle.

Good arguments are always available for redefining a market. We have found some variations and lack of clarity in the way most firms defined their 'market', with different departments seeing things in different ways. These discussions are needed *before* metrics are defined. The whole process loses meaning if the goalposts are moved. Accordingly, the metrics should always be accompanied by a description of what 'market' means and confirmation that it has not changed. From time to time, market definition *will* need to change, but then both versions should run in parallel so that comparisons are maintained until the transition is over.

Market share calculations also need care to ensure that the numerator and denominator (company's sales and total market sales) are at the same stage of distribution. In a Christmas seasonal business, for example, the peak sales *into* retailers will be in November but sales *out* to consumers will peak in December. Dividing the manufacturer's monthly sales turnover by total retail sales will therefore distort market share unless the pipeline effects are adjusted. Many industries share data, via some neutral service, so that all firms have like-for-like comparisons. When it works well, it is cheap and effective. But not always: after forty years of practice, the joint data collection system for the UK brewing sector still falls down.

Another solution is to measure, as Shell does, the share of consumer *preferences* brand by brand. This is more predictive than market share, but I prefer to see it as an indicator of brand equity – see below.

There must be well over a thousand different kinds of marketing measures. As managers cannot cope with more than a few, the Executive Summary introduced some more precise classification. Metrics are the key measures the board should see, e.g. sales turnover. Diagnostics are lower-level analyses of metrics, e.g. sales by product size, or sales by region. Diagnostics are needed, but not necessarily by the board, to explain variances in the metrics.

The trend in a metric, e.g. sales as a percentage of those in the previous year, receives little attention because it is assumed that any board will be looking at the trends anyway. *The size of any metric is less important than the way it is changing.* However, some will argue for the trend itself's being a brand equity measure, i.e. a brand equity that is growing is a better asset than one that is not. True enough, but a single metric is a snapshot and the trend is a 'derivative'. Thus the rate of growth of loyalty is a derivative. Sophisticates will also look at second-order derivatives, i.e. the rate of change in the trend. For example, is the increase in sales accelerating or slowing down? Trend analysis is crucial, but the metrics have to be in place first. As systems bed down, boards may wish to replace metrics by their derivatives.

Metrics should be precise (both in their shared meaning and in the way they are measured), consistent over time and also from place to place, necessary (i.e. no redundancy), sufficient (i.e. comprehensive) and aligned with the firm's objectives. The word 'metric' was selected less for its association with measurement than for its historic role as the rhythm in music. When the rhythm goes wrong or musicians choose their own tempi, disaster ensues.

The general approach

The idea of identifying just a few standard metrics that could be used by all companies has arisen frequently during discussions with marketers. They are not deterred by the difficulties companies such as IBM have had in securing internal agreement to a much longer list, or by the variety of 'top five' metrics the generalist advocates put forward. Nevertheless, we found consistent themes: sales and profit, own and relative measures and the need to balance internal financial numbers with consumer and customer preference.

IBM

IBM is the world's largest information technology company, with global revenues in 1998 of $81.7 billion, which is almost twice those of the second-largest company in the IT industry. Rated as the sixth-largest company in the Fortune 500, IBM is the world's largest vendor of computer hardware, and is the number one IT services company. About 70% of all the corporate data in the world is managed by IBM software, and most importantly IBM is the world leader in the provision and own use of internet technology and services. In 1999, IBM expects to transact between $10 billion and $15 billion of business via e-commerce.

Having been the undisputed leader of the IT industry for several decades up to the 1980s, IBM temporarily lost that position in the early '90s, when the pundits forecast the impending demise of IBM before a host of new, agile competitors. But the astonishing transformation of IBM and its re-establishment of leadership in the latter years of the '90s have become a case study in corporate reinvention. A major element of this 'miracle' has been the transformation of IBM from a 'sales-led' company to a 'marketing-led' company.

While IBM's entire business, from organization and management systems to infrastructural processes and 'go to market' models, has been reconstructed from a multinational model to a global model, no part of IBM has been more dramatically changed than marketing. Marketing is today core, and Abby Kohnstamm, Senior VP, Marketing, is a powerful member of the corporate executive team. Under her leadership, the 'IBM' brand has been re-established as one of the world's most recognized and most valued brands. From being a collection of largely autonomous and dispersed units, marketing is now a centrally managed, global operation utilizing computer-based standard processes covering all elements of the marketing cycle from market analysis and market planning, competitive analysis and product management to marketing communications. Market information, campaign measurement and marketing effectiveness are tracked against standardized metrics, and are electronically shared globally and instantaneously.

IBM is a leader in the application of technology to marketing, and is advanced in the use of data mining, database analytics and customer relationship management. The measurement of 'brand value' in the eyes of IBM's customers, partners and stakeholders is a continuous process, and customers' needs and preferences are the central and most influential factor in IBM's business and marketing strategies.

The future of marketing in IBM will be strongly influenced by, and will in turn help to shape, the blinding speed of development of the Internet. The networked world will create a revolution in marketing. IBM's term for the pervasive utilization of Web-based communication to and between all participants in the supply chain is 'e-business'. The global e-business advertising campaigns run by IBM in recent times have firmly established IBM as the leader in this field. Reaching and serving customers on the Net will enable marketers to obtain instant feedback and customer information, which promises to transform marketing from an imprecise art into an accurate and readily measurable science.

Source: Metrics interview with Mike Mawtus, Vice-President, IBM Euro Global Initiatives, autumn 1998.

A variety of techniques, e.g. Delphi,[1] can be employed to reduce measures to a manageable set. Ideally, past data is tracked to identify those few metrics that are non-duplicative, add new information and are predictive.

Measures that move in exact step can be reduced to a single measure or index. Professors Agarwal and Rao, for example, have found that ten popular brand equity measures (such as perceptions and attitudes, preferences, choice intentions, and actual choice) were convergent.[2] Perceptions, preference and intentions (five in all) predicted market share but 'all these brand equity constructs may be necessary to *fully* explain choice'. In other words, they were not similar enough to allow measures to be dropped altogether.

Another approach, although much more difficult, is to discover the metrics used by exemplar firms, whether they be immediate competitors or those similar enough to provide useful lessons. The metrics used by exemplar firms will reveal their implicit models of how shareholder value is extracted from their marketplaces. This competitive intelligence should not only refine your own firm's model but help develop differentiation, and thus competitive advantage.

The general approach breaks into two: financial indicators from the profit and loss account adjusted by brand equity changes (non-financial).

Financial metrics

For a single brand market segment, three financial metrics (top line, marketing investment and bottom line), when compared against both the marketing plan and competition, give an adequate overview of marketing performance *provided* brand equity is unchanged.

Table 3.1 shows how these three financial metrics are often used and Table 3.2 will later show the five top brand equity measures that apply to most companies.

Table 3.1 ▦ Standard P&L metrics

Actual metric	% compared with plan	% compared with competition	Board review frequency
Sales	Volume/value	Market share	Monthly
Marketing investment	Period costs	Share of voice	Quarterly
Bottom line	e.g. economic profit	Share of profit	Half-yearly *

*The board will review the *company's* bottom line, certainly monthly and maybe weekly, but this is the profit by *brand* market unit analysis.

Thus the three actual measures provide six comparisons that together give an overall assessment. The Metrics project has found that most companies also use comparisons with the prior year in order to try to distinguish planning errors from performance. In other words, where variances with plan are substantial, the plan itself may be at fault.

Some boards review sales daily, notably retail firms and small and medium-sized enterprises (SMEs). Others see them monthly. Few can, or wish to, obtain competitive data with the same frequency as internal data. The availability of market data can also vary from daily to weekly, monthly to annually or just *ad hoc* when the need arises. This lack of synchronization posed a problem for most of the firms we talked to and is a processing issue best left for later. Here we just assume that marketing cannot be assessed as a whole more often than monthly and that twice a year is enough for most companies. To continue the medical metaphor from previous chapters, this is like checking the pulse frequently but waiting for the doctor to visit before conducting the full health check. We just need to note that, without watching the market, internal data can mislead.

Brand equity

Having established three financial metrics, we now need to monitor changes in brand equity. This takes us back to the brand positioning statement and questions like:

- Do end users know what this brand is/does for them? (Awareness)

- Who are the target market, or what I prefer to call 'partner consumers'?

- Which is the target competitor? And market? (See above)

- Why is it different and better? (It cannot be better if it is not different first)

- How is that reinforced by the price positioning?

Andersen Consulting

Sarah McMahon is an Associate Partner with the team responsible for marketing the business itself, as distinct from that for advising clients. Andersen Consulting has led the way with innovative TV advertising and brand image campaigns. During 1999 they were working on a brand equity measurement initiative. With 65,000 staff worldwide, co-ordinating global marketing efforts is no mean task.

The objective of the initiative was to create a measurement tool that accurately reported AC's brand equity compared with the rest of the consulting market. They were concerned with the components to be measured and how, the competitors to be benchmarked and how the brand equity components could be combined to reduce the number of metrics.

After studying the academic and professional literature, eight components were selected:

- Inclusion in the consideration set
- Awareness
- Preference
- Consultant attributes
- Personality traits
- Perceived capability
- Corporate image
- Satisfaction.

Data was collected at a more detailed level and analyzed to identify the factors making up each component. Benchmarking of each factor showed clear competitive differences. The data was also aggregated to provide an overall 'Brand Equity Score'. An important conclusion from this initiative was that the brand equity model should be incorporated into the firm's 'Marketing & Communications Scorecard'.

Source: Metrics interview with Sarah McMahon, November 1999.

Many metrics can quickly be generated from the positioning questions above. Here we search for potential universals, leaving goal-driven metrics to the next section. The five brand equity indicators that follow are concepts. Exactly how each is measured will vary according to sector and data availability. The five are:

- Relative satisfaction
- Commitment
- Relative perceived quality
- Relative price
- Availability.

Consumer satisfaction has been one of the fastest-growing metrics worldwide. In the UK, 68% of companies use it, 36% of boardrooms see it and 46% of our middle management respondents rated it as a very important measure. However, doubts have been raised about its sensitivity. When surveyed, some customers claim to be satisfied and then switch to another brand. Others claim dissatisfaction and stay loyal. Empirical US research has shown that a better metric is *relative* satisfaction, i.e. relative to market or key competitor(s):[3] however much consumers *like* Brand A, they may leave if they like Brand B *more*.

Inertia, lack of information, lack of product experience and the cost of changing all explain why consumers stay with Brand A even though they prefer Brand B, which is why *relative* satisfaction is a better measure than satisfaction alone. This is particularly important for financial services, such as banks, where consumers change only with reluctance. This suggests that the prime candidate for brand equity assessment is relative consumer satisfaction, or preference.

How does this fit in with 'awareness', the first question companies often ask about their brands? Awareness is the most-used marketing measure at 78% but appears in only 28% of boardrooms, and only 28% of our respondents rated it as a very important measure. Research by Young and Rubicam shows that awareness is a vital indicator for new brands but, as they mature, awareness proves nothing much. Furthermore, it is implied by satisfaction/preference, since if one is not aware of it, one is unlikely to be satisfied by it. That, however, does not reduce the role of awareness as a *diagnostic* within satisfaction analysis.

The second brand equity candidate tests the *depth* of satisfaction or preference, i.e. **commitment**. Specific measures of commitment, expressed as the likelihood of switching, are now available. This is more than differentiation, which is also prompted by brand positioning, but is perhaps more of a diagnostic than a metric. After all, if the brand is not seen as different, customers are unlikely to be committed to it. Commitment measures the propensity of customers to stay with the brand, and thus it is seen as a firm-specific rather than a relative (to other brands) metric.

Loyalty, whether over successive time periods or expressed as a share of category requirements within one period, does not necessarily imply deep commitment. It may just be habit. Customer retention, a key measure in many sectors such as financial services, is also a measure of loyalty, though retail banks have discovered that that also may be more habit than satisfaction. Telecoms companies use churn as the negative equivalent. Relevance to the consumer, purchase intention and 'bonding', a WPP metric, are all also seen as potential indicators of commitment.

Any of these will serve as proxies if commitment cannot be directly measured. Better still, all candidate indicators, including commitment itself, can be tested against subsequent sales and brand equity metrics if the data is available.

As noted above, the selection of the precise form of calculation, even for these general metrics, needs to be determined by sector relevance and data availability.

Relative perceived quality has been shown to be superior to market share as a predictor of future profits.[4] In practice the absolute indicator, 'perceived quality' or 'esteem', is used more often than the comparative. In our research, 64% of companies used it, 32% at boardroom level, and 35% of respondents gave it a top billing for assessing marketing performance. As with satisfaction, both the absolute and relative metrics should be interesting to the board, but the competitive indicator is likely to provide a better forecast of subsequent performance. Share of preference, which some see as a better indicator than market share, is likely to be highly correlated with relative perceived quality and may be a suitable near-match alternative. It is worth comparing the data.

Relative price is easier to measure as it is simply the annual market share (value) divided by the market share (volume), although it is affected by how one defines the market. Using short time periods to compare prices with some competitors is open to manipulation. In our research, relative price was one of the favourite indicators (it ranked 7 among all marketing metrics and 3 among non-financial metrics): it was used by 70% of companies, 34% at boardroom level, while 37% of respondents saw it as a top performance metric. Relative price should match perceived quality and, if all is well, should therefore be redundant. As with other brand equity measures, or human health checks come to that, it needs to be monitored precisely because if perceived quality and relative price are out of line – especially if quality is falling while price is rising – a major problem exists. If it has not yet hit the top line P&L metric, it will.

Availability is usually measured by trade distribution but, as the interface between the two, it is treated here as a consumer measure. Preference is expressed at this level by whether the brand is stocked or not.

Distribution, usually weighted by store volume or turnover, is used (as a proxy for availability) by 66% of UK firms. But only 11% of boards see this metric and only 18% of respondents regarded it as very important for overall assessment. Nielsen has traditionally supplied this data to grocery-sector marketers along with diagnostics such as region and out-of-stocks. More sophisticated distribution measures take the extent of the brand range into account. For example, if each brand has ten flavours available in three sizes, it has 30 SKUs (stock-keeping units). If 100% of retail outlets handle just one flavour in one size, this is probably less attractive than 50% of outlets each handling the full 30 SKUs. The arithmetic here can be complex, as it turns on the relative sales potential of each SKU in each store. Non-moving SKUs are no help to anyone.

Availability has less support than the other metrics. Accountants are especially unconvinced by this measure. It is also double-edged in the sense that more is not necessarily better. The required distribution has to be part of the brand's positioning. The majority view is that availability belongs to the tailored approach, not the shortlist, or that it is more of a diagnostic than a metric. Even so, I have retained it *because a false reading can be given by the other figures without it*. Increased sales and static measures of relative satisfaction, commitment, relative perceived quality and relative price would imply success but may be explained by growing availability without any consumer uptake. Similar arguments can be applied to **pipeline** (the number of days of stock in trade, i.e. sold by the brand owner but not yet bought by the consumer). Marlboro Friday immortalized one of the most dramatic price cuts of all time. On 2 April 1993 Philip Morris cut the lead cigarette prices in the US by 20% and the share price fell pro rata. While the relative price had been allowed to creep higher than perceived quality, the latter was the bigger problem. Philip Morris had allowed the pipeline – which they were not tracking at senior levels – to be overstocked. Tobacco has a short shelf life. Nevertheless, availability has wider implications than over- or understocking and, as the far more prevalent indicator, is here preferred.

In summary, changes in brand equity could be assessed from the increase or decrease in the metrics in Table 3.2.

Table 3.2 ■ General brand equity metrics

Consumer metric	Measured by
Relative satisfaction	Consumer preference or satisfaction as per cent average for market/ competitor(s). The competitive benchmark should be stated
Commitment	Index of switchability (or some similar measure of retention, loyalty, purchase intent or bonding)
Relative perceived quality	Perceived quality satisfaction as per cent average for market/ competitor(s). The competitive benchmark should be stated
Relative price	Market share (value)/Market share (volume)
Availability	Distribution, e.g. weighted percentage of retail outlets carrying the brand

The importance of consistent market definition, noted after Table 3.1, applies here too, as does the need for consistency in defining the end user segment. When metrics are presented at board level, the brand market segment unit of analysis should be reaffirmed and any variations treated as outlined above, i.e. both sets should be presented until the transition is complete.

Thus our five measures of brand equity must be seen as the year-on-year change in the marketing asset. This change adjusts the performance revealed by the three P&L measures when compared with the internal goals for that BMS and competitive benchmarks.

This general 3+5 (P&L + brand equity) approach has drawn on universal marketing basics. We now turn to the alternative: metrics drawn from, and tailored to, the firm's objectives.

The tailored approach

The standard creative briefs for new advertising campaigns do not include space for what measurable effect(s) the advertising should achieve.[5] They do detail the media to be used and what the ads should say, but that is like telling a plumber what tools to use without telling him where the leak is. In the same way, identifying the metrics to be used is difficult unless you first identify the problem(s) the marketing is supposed to solve.

The importance of metrics may lie less in control and more in the clear direction they imply for managers throughout the firm. The most important planning question is also the simplest: how will we recognize success when we see it? This is the box which should be added to every advertising creative brief in the world, along with board approval of any business or marketing plan.

In this respect, leadership, direction, strategy and measurement are all aspects of the same concept. Alignment prevents the confusion of signals. The overriding justification for metrics is their value as pointers to what the company seeks to achieve and as milestones along that path.

This is why the tailored approach is the antithesis of the general. To succeed, a firm must have a different strategy and, to some extent, that implies different metrics. If it chooses the same measures as everyone else, its thinking risks becoming standardized. ACNeilsen sells syndicated information to direct competitors who are more likely to respond in similar ways, precisely because they see the same information. Competitive metrics like market share and share of voice help to show who is winning, but the thinking is still trammelled in the conventional. Higher relative consumer satisfaction is good, but if everyone is attacking the same target the returns are likely to be low.

In marketing, the extremes of conventionality and differentiation are both sub-optimal. Consumers want their products to be familiar and easy to use and yet different enough to be distinguished and better. Board members are likely to increase marketing conformity if their social ties are with others in the same sector. For example, is it a good thing for them to spend more time with their trade associations? Economists since Adam Smith have viewed these associations with suspicion, but leaving market management aside, do those social contacts promote conventional marketing? Professors Marta Geletkanycz of Boston and Donald Hambrick of Columbia considered that they did, along with other forms of intra-sector relationships such as cross-board representation, at least by comparison with board members who cast their social nets beyond their immediate trade sector.[6] It turned out that the strategic conformists' (association attenders') companies did better under trading conditions of high uncertainty whereas more stable environments suited the deviants better.

It follows that the extent of strategic differentiation/conformity should be a matter of conscious board choice depending on the trading environment and competition.

A few years ago, the Chartered Institute of Marketing commissioned London Business School to examine the return on marketing expenditure in the financial services industry.[7] In effect we were invited to determine the *efficiency* of marketing expenditure in terms of the increased profits it contributed. We were not able to do this across the sample because of lack of data. The firms themselves could not do so either. What we did find was *effectiveness*: by and large firms were achieving the targets in their plan. Competitive firms were winning because they were setting different targets, i.e. metrics. In the Metrics project research we also found that management is increasingly assigning more importance to effectiveness than efficiency

Determining goals and then measuring and reporting on success against them is a key part of organizational learning. Failures, as always, are more valuable for this purpose than success. And multinationals have the extra advantage of sharing this information globally. McDonald's gives a good example of a disciplined and advanced approach to measurement as the primary basis for global learning. It believes in keeping with the basics but building its database to provide sophisticated forecasts and diagnostics.

McDonald's

Nuala Cahalan is responsible for brand and product research at McDonald's, which employs 50–60,000 people in the UK. Marketing controls all the classic four Ps and drives the business with the support of other departments. There are four key areas for metrics. Sales transactions have equal priority with customer satisfaction and functional elements such as value for money and cleanliness. The second set are market share and brand equity measures such as awareness and advertising recall and mystery diners who assess their whole visits. Brand equity was introduced five or six years earlier and is becoming increasingly important.

Marketing is assessed quarterly by top management against pre-set targets for these measures. The future looks to better models using better segmentation and providing more actionable and precise information. Accordingly, the company is moving from the 'market-focus' stage of evolution to the 'scientific'.

Source: Metrics interview by Sashi Halve with Nuala Cahalan, 12 April 1999.

Most of our Metrics project respondents regarded it as axiomatic that metrics should flow from strategy, but it may sometimes be easier to do it the other way round: to deduce the strategy from the measures the board likes to see. The mail order firm Freemans, for example, has a promotional, rather than a strategic, marketing focus.

Freemans

At the time of this interview with Michael Cutbill, Marketing Director, Freemans was still part of Sears plc and second-largest in the traditional mail order industry behind Kays (GUS). Although Cutbill reports directly to the MD, marketing is not a board position. Marketing is seen as what the marketing department does.

Freemans, like the rest of the industry, does not aim to build its brand directly through advertising but to improve promotional effectiveness and increase the size of the customer base. The promotions aim to encourage customers to get the catalogue out again. Of course, increasing penetration and purchase frequency does then build the brand.

Metrics are specific to catalogue-driven marketing and therefore unlike fmcg (packaged goods). Key ratios are the size of the database, the active percentage of buyers, seasonality, promotional effects and profiles of buyers.

Source: Metrics interview with Michael Cutbill, Marketing Director, 30 December 1998.

Where the firm's market strategy is explicit, the metrics should select themselves. Consumer segments and retention versus gaining new consumers will have been prioritized, for example. Push (through the channel) will have been balanced with pull. The expectations from direct customers and outside influencers, e.g. trade journalists, will have been formed, if not quantified.

Conversely, where the metrics are established, the strategy can be deduced. Of course, neither may be true but the situation is easy to test. Appendix B lists the top 37 metrics found in our research. Which are relevant to your firm? Does your strategy imply that the metric should be monitored or, if not, does the relevance of the metric imply that you should have a strategy dealing with that aspect of your business? Or would any result on that metric be acceptable?

Selecting metrics from the existing popular favourites is practical but not profound. In the absence of something more radical it is a good place to start, but it should promote questions such as 'Would more be better for us?' For example, increasing awareness for a small new entrepreneur would almost certainly be positive even if the reasons for the awareness were not. The first stage is just getting known. On the other hand, many people only became aware of Monsanto as a result of the genetically modified foods scare. The increase in awareness was not only unnecessary for such a well-established firm that was already held in high regard by its target markets, but was damaging to the extent that the company considered changing its name.

Similarly, most managers regard more market share as better, but they may be wrong. More share bought at the expense of reputation, e.g. through price promotions, can damage the brand's health permanently. The French have established special skills with prestige brands, such as particular fashion items, perfumes and alcoholic beverages (e.g. cognac). Any of these brands could double their market share if they wished, but through 'vulgarisation'. In other words, if the brands become too popular they lose their cachet, and ultimately their *raison d'être*.

So run the firm's strategy trolley round the metrics supermarket and see which metrics fit in. That preliminary analysis should quickly inform the board about some incremental improvements that could be made both to strategy and to the metrics in use. The more profound question is perhaps for the board's next annual strategy retreat: does this match of strategy and metrics fully describe the success we are seeking? Inevitably some things will be missing and some things will need to be changed, but the point here is that the tailored approach to metrics and strategy formulation is interactive: metrics are not just an afterthought.

In particular, the board should consider where its brand(s) should be on the conformity/deviancy scales. Where is the consumer looking for comfort and where for differentiation and innovation? Measuring innovation health forms a later chapter, but I found it odd that differentiation was so rarely used as a metric. Perhaps, commitment serves as a proxy, but that needs to be tested.

Compared to what?

The general and the tailored approaches have been separated for the sake of analysis. In practice, firms evolve their metrics in the light of the firm's experience and that of newcomers. Radical restructuring from a clean sheet is rare. One of the reasons for this is the need for comparison and therefore continuity.

As noted above, trends matter more than the metrics themselves. Comparing metrics with planned targets is ideal, but the targets themselves must have come from somewhere – hopefully a mix of past experience and what the competition is achieving, or is likely to achieve.

Serving metrics without comparisons is as messy as serving spaghetti without a plate. Without a stable base, loose ends will be flying all over the place. Shell provides an interesting case history of using different methods for comparison.

Figuring the Ferrari sponsorship

How much Shell spends on sponsoring Ferrari for Formula 1 is a closely guarded secret. Needless to say, Shell's top management is keen to know the financial justification for this expenditure. Prior to signing a new five-year sponsorship contract, Shell evaluated the costs and benefits in a number of different ways. They took the view that no one method could give an exact answer, but that a range of methodologies taken together would provide the range of answers.

In principle, sponsorship is similar to advertising, so their first approach was to compare the attitudes towards the Shell brand of those who were aware of the Ferrari link with that of those who were not. There are two assumptions here, which probably cancel each other out. Reporting awareness underestimates those who were, in fact, influenced by the sponsorship but have since forgotten about it. On the other hand, those already favourable to Shell are more likely to be aware of the promotion. Using existing conversion rates, this difference in attitudes could be translated into extra sales and then profits. Specifically, share of preference (a more sensitive measure than market share) was converted, for those calculated to have shifted, to the total effect on share and then sales and incremental profit.

The second method was similar but used the measured change in purchasing behaviour rather than the shift in attitudes.

The third methodology involved an independent assessment by a brand valuation expert. This included branding, sales, price premium and advertising effects.

The fourth approach is perhaps the most interesting. Different Shell companies had merchandised the sponsorship to varying extents in their different countries. If the sponsorship was essentially profitable then those who used it more fully should have reaped more profit. Conversely, if it was intrinsically unprofitable then, the more they spent on it the more they should have lost. These country-to-country comparisons revealed a positive picture, i.e. the investment paid off, as well as showing that the laggards should be more forward in future.

The final method was a form of the Delphi[8] technique. Managers were surveyed for their opinions based on their experience but without being given any new evidence. This showed they were highly skewed, rating the sponsorship very high or very low in terms of their perceived return on investment. They were also asked for their arguments for and against the sponsorship. These responses were used to help guide the market research terms of the questions to be answered. In a second wave, managers were provided wit the evidence from the market research and the for/against question was asked again. Other than in some technical areas such as aviation (not so relevant), the responses we now overwhelmingly favourable.

The results of all these approaches were drawn together in a short slide presentatio for the top executive team, who then approved the new five-year contract.

Metrics can provide indication of both effectiveness (did we achieve goals?) and efficiency (did we do so with least resources?). Efficiency is usually shown by return on investment. Pan-company marketing may not be separable from the total business for the purposes of assessing efficiency. Advertising and promotional assessment can, in principle, include efficiency, but that is covered in Appendix A.

So we are mostly concerned with effectiveness, and the metrics only give half the picture. The other half is the quality of the benchmarks against which the metrics are compared. Not long ago, a company achieved 93%, 98% and 104% of sales targets during the same period. No, this was not three separate brands but three separate targets for the same brand market segment. Only the goalposts moved.

Faced by this reforecasting experience, some companies stick with prior year, or use outside comparisons such as total market or identified competitors. Each of these has its adherents, but best practice is for the targets to be set by the annual planning process. That is what it is for. The after-the-fact disclaimer that the plan was wrong is unacceptable: all plans turn out to be wrong. Their role is to describe what will be achieved and how. Only the most volatile markets negate the value of some formal planning, however rudimentary.

The first moral, of course, is that these plan benchmarks for later metric comparison need to be tested thoroughly before they are accepted. The second moral is that the achievement, or otherwise, of these period goals is only part of the story. Boards should also be given comparisons with prior years (perhaps in graphical form) and with competitors.

Executive minutes 3

1 Finance director to report on the presentation of the three basic profit and loss measures of marketing performance for each brand market segment (sales, marketing investment and bottom line) compared to the current system. Are the three metrics compared with plan and competition? Should they also be compared with prior year?

2 Marketing team to compare the five general consumer brand equity measures (relative satisfaction, commitment, relative perceived quality, relative price, and availability) with existing measures and report on whether the general measures are adequate. If not, what should be added/subtracted?

3 Board to receive task force presentation on how a long list of metrics (those in Appendix B plus existing metrics plus those adapted from other sources) compares with the firm's strategic objectives and which mix of general and tailored metrics best fits the firm. Task force to check data availability.

4 Board to revisit the question 'What will success look like?' Part of the next annual strategy retreat to be devoted to reviewing strategy and the metrics that will indicate progress in that direction.

5 Board to determine benchmarks for metric comparison and how they should be presented.

References

1 In the 'Delphi' technique, a group of experts separately provide solutions (often forecasts), which are then merged. The group discusses the similarities and variances, and the reasons for those differences. Then each expert independently provides a solution and the merger and discussion cycle takes place again. In theory this leads to robust convergence to the 'best' answer. It is similar to IGI (individual, then group, then individual) brainstorming.

2   Agarwal, Manoj K. and Rao, Vithala R. (1996) 'An empirical comparison of consumer-based measures of brand equity', *Marketing Letters* 7 (3), 237–47.

3   Ryan, Michael J.; Rayner, Robert and Morrison, Andy (1999) 'Diagnosing customer loyalty drivers', *Marketing Research* 11 (2: summer), 18–26.

Varki, Sajeev and Rust, Roland T. (1997) 'Satisfaction is relative', *Marketing Research* 9 (2: summer), 14–19.

Vredenburg, Harrie and Wee Chow-Hou (1986) 'The role of customer service in determining customer satisfaction', *Journal of the Academy of Marketing Science* 14 (2: summer), 17–26.

4   Gale, Bradley T. (1994) *Managing Customer Value*, New York: Free Press.

5   Survey of advertising agency creative brief proformas, April 2000.

6   Geletkanycz, Marta A.S. and Hambrick, Donald C. (1997) 'The external ties of top executives: implications for strategic choice and performance', *Administrative Science Quarterly* 42 (Dec), 654–81.

7   Swartz, Gordon; Hardie, Bruce; Grayson, Kent and Ambler, Tim. (1996) 'Value for money? The relationships between marketing expenditure and business performance in the UK financial services industry', *Chartered Institute of Marketing*, April.

8   See note 1 above.

4

Stages of assessing marketing performance

So far we have looked at why firms should assess their marketing performance at the highest level; we have assessed the central role of brand equity and have considered how to go about selecting the right metrics. Now we take a more detailed look at the process of performance assessment itself. As with other company processes, it evolves and does not spring, ready-formed, from some consultant's drawing board. Use this chapter to help decide where your company is on the evolutionary scale, and how best you can move along it.

This chapter covers the following key points (see also Figure 4.1):

- What the five stages of marketing assessment are;
- The balance between financial and non-financial measures at board level;
- Promoting consistency through alignment of goals, brand market segments and metrics.

In brief, the advice will be to:

- Decide what stage you are at and then progress rapidly;
- Take each stage in turn;
- Balance financial and non-financial market measures;
- Harmonize the internal system for monthly and (semi-)annual assessments;

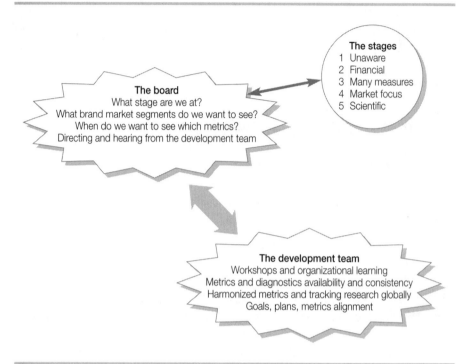

Fig 4.1 ■ Stages of assessing marketing performance

■ Use segmentation to develop the brand market units into brand market segments as the units for marketing assessment;

■ Align goals and metrics for each assessment unit.

The five stages of marketing assessment

The Metrics research has found that most companies develop their thinking about overall marketing assessment, and specifically the marketing asset, in five stages:

1 The company is **unaware of the issue**. Marketing is not seen as something requiring the formal attention of the main board.

2 Assessment is seen in terms of **financial evaluation**. Commercial matters for board attention need to be expressed as money. The board will review marketing, but only in terms of profit and loss account and cash flow, and perhaps brand valuation.

3 Assessment is seen as requiring **many measures**. The company recognizes that money is too limiting a vocabulary. A multitude of non-financial measures come into use. A diversity of measures is used by different departments, some of which are extracted for board attention.

4 The company develops **market focus**. Management streamlines the variety of financial and non-financial metrics to give a single coherent view of the market.

5 A **scientific** method of assessment is adopted. The database of past and current metrics, derivatives and diagnostics is mathematically analyzed to provide the shortest list of sensitive and predictive metrics.

While companies might benefit from bypassing one or more stages, leaping evolutionary stages compromises organizational learning. Pan-company marketing, by definition, concerns everyone, and therefore everyone, not just the board, should understand what marketing is supposed to be achieving and whether it is doing so. When the building society Bradford and Bingley (see case study in Chapter 1) moved from the financial stage to making the customer central, it set up a series of workshops for each business unit to define functional mission and goals, and associated critical success factors and performance measures. Managing this evolution has a number of benefits: it promotes market orientation throughout the company and signals the priorities from the very top about what will, or should, be measured.

Of course, in practice, this evolution is not as neat as a steady progression through the five stages may seem. Some companies, following a change of management perhaps, move back from the 'many measures' stage to that of 'financial evaluation'. Others, like Boots, the retail health and beauty care chain, do both at the same time.

Boots

Lord Blyth, as Chief Executive and then Executive Chairman, has been leading the value-based management (VBM) movement for ten years, both in the company and as a role model in the UK as a whole. Accordingly some might see Boots as a financially driven business, though the company itself would see VBM as more broadly defining the way to manage a business and taking market perspectives into account in shaping the strategy of each business unit. Indeed it sees each business unit as customer-driven and marketing-aligned accordingly. Clearly both work together, though our orientation questions placed the owners, i.e. shareholders, well ahead of customers in terms of primacy.

Overall there is perhaps a 70/30 emphasis on efficiency, e.g. return on marketing investment, over effectiveness, e.g. achieving strategic goals. This dichotomy may be false as both are crucial. Innovation, for example, is a strategic priority for the Boots group and a director of innovation has recently been appointed.

Competitive measures are also important both at corporate level, where total shareholder returns are compared with both UK and global peers, and at business unit level. Boots the Chemist's key competitors are the food superstore operators (such as Tesco and Asda) and Superdrug.

Source: Metrics interview with Mike Dutton, Head of Corporate Analysis, 30 October 1998. Revised 23 June 1999.

Stage one: unaware of the issue

In the first stage, the idea of assessing marketing performance has simply not arisen. For most British companies, the revelation that they are marketers is like Molière's M. Jourdain discovering that he had been speaking prose for forty years.

For many others, the annual cycle of plans may be so ritualized as to attract no critical marketing review. If the company is profitable and doing well in the market, it may wish to leave well alone, ignoring the fact that markets can change to the company's detriment overnight.

When making things was the problem, companies were rightly preoccupied with supply issues. Demand was there to be met. Today this is less true. Production is mechanized and can be sourced from any part of the globe. Men released from factories and agriculture and women released from their homes have increased the numbers available for service-sector employment. Certain skills are ever short but employees, as a whole, are not. And nor is supply.

Thus while costs remain an issue, the focus has shifted from supply to demand. Companies of all kinds are becoming more concerned with revenue growth and, more importantly, growth in profitable sectors and segments. In Britain, for example, Hugh Davidson, author of *Even More Offensive Marketing*, recognizing the reluctance of firms to embrace the term 'marketing', has suggested replacing it by 'demand management'.

And reluctance there is. While a number of our respondents in the Metrics project described how their companies had emerged from this unaware stage, other reports have shown that marketing is either ignored or deplored in many British companies. Only a minority have formal marketing functions or board representation. And marketing tops the list of expenditure most likely to be cut when times are hard.[1] In 1999, finance directors considered that marketing budgets were at least twice as likely to be cut as human resources, training, and research and development, with IT being ten times less likely. Worryingly, the disregard for marketing had increased since the previous survey in 1996. In both surveys the sample was 100 finance and 100 marketing directors drawn from *The Times'* top 1,000 companies.

From the same KPMG survey, only just over half the finance directors saw marketing as a necessary investment for long-term growth. See Table 4.1.

Table 4.1 ■ Long-term investment priorities for finance directors

'To what degree do you see the following as a necessary investment for long-term growth?'	1999 %	1996 %
Information technology	92	91
Training	86	94
Human resources	79	79
Research and development	59	73
Marketing	57	58

Perhaps of greater concern was that only 82% of marketing directors saw marketing investment as necessary.

Our telephone surveys of members of The Marketing Society and senior chartered accountants revealed that the main market metrics were seen by only one-third of their boards – and this sample is biased to the larger, more marketing-aware companies. We can say without equivocation that the great majority of British companies are at this 'unaware' stage. For a lucky few, demand and the market take care of themselves. For everyone else, market performance is the crucial determinant of success, and yet most ignore it.

On the positive side, Centrica is one example of the many companies that have developed rapidly from the unaware to the later stages.

Centrica

Simon Waugh is Group Director of Marketing at Centrica, which is the customer-facing part of British Gas. It trades and supplies gas and electricity for both consumers and businesses, has created a financial services business, e.g. Goldfish credit cards, and has retail stores. It was engineering-led and, perhaps as a result, measures 90% of what it does, including marketing.

Its priorities for metrics are, first, customer satisfaction, both behavioural and attitudinal, financial performance, competitive indicators and then innovation. Customer service is 'measured stringently'. Marketing-mix models are used for assessing advertising and promotion. These measures are forecasted in plans and later compared with what actually happens. All this is a major departure from the traditional monopoly approach of five years previously.

Given the plethora of measures, Centrica regards itself as being at the 'many' stage of metrics evolution. Notwithstanding all the changes, tradition and loyalty run high. Controls are strong but so is commitment.

Source: Metrics interview with Simon Waugh, 28 October 1998.

Stage two: financial evaluation

Difficulties in affording and setting marketing budgets typically lead to questions of return on marketing investment and/or expenditure. As well as financial returns within the period as shown by the profit and loss account, marketers and accountants may look to financial valuation of brand equity.

Most large companies assessing marketing are seeking financial solutions. They have many market measures, which are most often costs, but they are used on a case-by-case basis to manage the mix within the marketing budget. They are not taken together for the purpose of overall marketing assessment. One or two senior respondents to the Metrics project, in fact, expressed surprise that they should share such measures with the board.

This 'black box' approach to marketing has much to commend it on the surface. The board remains concerned with the financial inputs, the costs and investment, and the outputs, i.e. the bottom line, and is not concerned with what happens in between. Some respondents even went so far as to attribute their success to keeping their boards out of marketing issues.

Similarly, some group board directors have told us that they see marketing as an operational matter that should be reviewed only by subsidiary boards. The top holding company should deal with strategy, including mergers and acquisitions, shareholders and overall financial issues. They should not, they believe, be concerned with customers and other local matters. This is especially true for those companies operating worldwide in many sectors with a wide range of brands. If they even began to consider individual brand market segment issues, they would never be done.

These views, while worthy, are naïve. For the reasons discussed in the Executive Summary, directors should make it their business to understand the sources of revenue. Such understanding requires more than noticing that money turns up from customers from time to time.

Multi-brand, multi-market firms do indeed face complexity in unravelling the market measures that matter. But one of the largest and most byzantine groups, Nestlé, provides an example of how these difficulties can be overcome. Note that it has allowed more divisional flexibility over measurement than others, such as IBM, permit. Sector, corporate culture and product diversity all play their parts in these decisions.

Nestlé

Much of the change to Nestlé's corporate structure over the last ten years has been driven by acquisitions such as Carnation, Buitoni, Perrier and Rowntree Mackintosh. The business now has four sector divisions – confectionery, beverages, food and ice cream. As a very successful marketer over many years, marketing is left to sector division management although the main strategic brands operate within frameworks established by the Head Office in Switzerland. The group has 8,500 brands worldwide and the main strategic ones are reported to headquarters in Vevey in a set format. The management committee has access to these reports but otherwise metrics are not consistent. Each division chooses how to measure its business. Inevitably there are many similarities.

While some see it more or less broadly, 'marketing' means what the marketing departments do. Two major areas of change concern trade promotions and advertising. The tendency to allocate ever more of the brand budget to the trade will be reviewed for brand impact and effectiveness. Advertising will migrate toward major strategic brands to spread the cost. That in turn will cause some brands to receive less support and others to receive a boost.

The marketing asset is not formalized but performance is closely benchmarked against competition. Perhaps surprisingly for one of the world's largest brand marketers, marketing assessment is at the 'financial' stage of evolution. Efficiency has a slight edge over effectiveness. Perhaps this reflects Nestlé's inherent conservatism with its emphasis on loyalty, tradition and commitment. The corporate head is seen as a mentor or parent figure more than a risk taker or a hard driver.

Source: Metrics interview with David Hudson, Communications and Corporate Affairs Director, 27 November 1998.

The three main approaches to reducing complexity and enabling boards to come to terms with their marketing assets and how to value them are:

- Reducing the sheer number of brands. Note how Procter & Gamble and Unilever have been selling off their less important brands.

- Putting more products under mega-brand names such as Nestlé and Pillsbury.

■ Selecting the key brand market units that make up the bulk of shareholder value. Rationalizing down to core businesses and brands. Profits may be reduced but shareholder value is enhanced by disposal of peripheral activities.

Despite the imperative to understand markets and the flaws in brand valuation, the financial evaluation stage has much to commend it. It is better than being unaware and it gets marketing on to the board table. Top boards are comfortable with financial measures: they put marketing investment on a par with capital expenditure and also evaluate everything even-handedly in terms of profits and/or cash flow.

Of course, one can operate both a financial and a market measures system in parallel. Cadbury, long a top marketing and brands business, has recently instituted state-of-the-art financial disciplines alongside marketing measures.

Cadbury

Developing famous brands is at the heart of Cadbury as a business. Marketing performance is closely tracked by the Cadbury Ltd board, the Confectionery stream board and Group Cadbury-Schweppes plc board. Marketing-to-sales ratios, share of voice and market share are all key performance indicators for the business. Advertising performance is tracked via Millward Brown and the average weight of purchase via Taylor Nelson. Performance in the marketplace is discussed at every board meeting.

The company has a 'marketing culture' where people from all round the organization suggest ideas, but marketing plans and programmes remain the accountability of the marketing/new product development/consumer knowledge team.

John Sunderland, the Group Chief Executive, has introduced the governing objective of maximizing shareholder value and this is underpinned by value-based management; this is a rigorous way of assessing which markets to compete in and how to achieve competitive advantage.

Key measures include performance against strategic milestones, market share, advertising spend, brand and advertising awareness, penetration and average weight of purchase and percentage of total volume accounted for by new products.

The profitability of brands is reviewed by the board regularly.

Source: Metrics interview with Sue Wall, Marketing Controller (Consumer Knowledge), 18 November 1998.

However, as the board gains confidence in the financial evaluation stage and its links to financial analysis of other activities, it becomes time to move on.

Stage three: many measures

Metrics project respondents at this stage have recognized that financial (mostly internal) measures need to be balanced by non-financial measures, including those from the marketplace (see the Bass example earlier). They have a plethora of marketing indicators, which are used for many different purposes. Their information systems have improved, and new market research has been added as new services have become available. Marketers always have a great appetite for knowledge about their markets. The AA is a good example.

Automobile Association

Bob Sinclair, at the time of the interview Group Marketing Director of the Automobile Association, has a 30-strong marketing team dealing mainly with brand ownership/ management, database management and specialist services like research and media. The AA, now part of Centrica, is an enthusiastic measurer: 'Everything we do we measure.'

The emphasis is now on direct response advertising and relationship marketing (whether subscribers renew). As the market saturates, market share is becoming increasingly important.

In Sinclair's view, innovation, while seen as important, is not high enough on the company's agenda and the bias toward efficiency over effectiveness should be evened out.

Sinclair sees the AA, a very large organization collecting and reporting a wide variety of measures, as being at the 'many measures' stage of evolution.

Source: Metrics interview with Bob Sinclair, Group Marketing Director, 1 December 1998.

The problem is that the copious availability of data can be overwhelming: it has been likened to sipping from a fire hydrant with its massive force of water. Nor is it unknown for managers to commission new research because it would take too long to find the same information somewhere in-house. And that in-house data is not always dependable. Steve Willis, of AXA Sun Life, recounts that, in the course of auditing IT systems for a manufacturing company, he found a monthly report used by the finance director for key decisions where the grand totals missed out the *leading* digit. In other words, the £ million figure was missing but the lower numbers were correct. The report had been happily used (or not used) for quite a long time. No doubt we all have similar tales.

So, as new demands and questions are raised, market research and internal measures increase faster than they are culled. Moreover, those charged with collecting information like to keep data coming, as they never know what questions will be asked next and because historical comparisons will be needed.

The variety of possible measures is endless. Wharton's Professor Marshall Meyer cites 117 measures in use by Skandia, the Swedish financial services firm.[2] The more the marketing effort is segmented by customer type and the more that other audiences are recognized (e.g. employees) the more measures there are likely to be. For each audience or segment one should consider both their expressed behaviours – what they do – and intermediate measures of their awareness – what they think and feel about the brand. These can all be provided as absolute measures, or relative to the market and/or specific competitors. Then they can be provided as graphs or charts to show comparisons over time.

In understandable reaction to surfeit, a demand exists for one single measure that will summarize the many. Brand valuation is the most frequent candidate but, as we considered in Chapter 2, no single indicator or index will serve. We need to look for signs of ill health and they are many. Whether in reaction to an attempt to use a single measure or just because it makes sense, marketers, at this stage, assemble a variety of financial and non-financial market and internal indicators for the board.

Duracell

The company was acquired by Gillette in 1996, which led to centralized marketing activities for Europe. The main group brands are now Oral B, Braun, Duracell and Gillette itself. Duracell is the leader in the fragmented UK batteries market with over 40% of the market share.

'Marketing' is seen as pan-company with everyone working towards the best products for the consumer. Marketing performance assessment for the UK is complicated by many activities', e.g. advertising, now being co-ordinated at global and European levels. Accordingly, financial measures dominate, with trade customer, then consumer, competitive and innovation measures following in turn. Nevertheless innovation is seen as important, with every business being charged with introducing at least one major innovation per year.

The marketing asset is termed 'brand equity', which is reviewed formally once a year though some measures are ongoing. The evolutionary stage is moving from 'many' to 'market focus'.

Source: Metrics interview with Stephen Tennant, then Customer Marketing Manager, now Business Unit Director (Duracell), UK, 21 December 1998.

There is a major difference between large companies and small and medium-sized enterprises that should be noted here: as a general rule, large companies have too much data and SMEs have too little.

Stage four: market focus

Sooner or later, senior management will demand a radical reassessment of what information truly matters. The beverage alcohol, Pillsbury and Burger King company, Diageo, for example, uses only about twenty measures in its 'Brand Equity Monitor'. Traditional profit and loss indicators, such as sales and profitability, balance consumer and competitive metrics. Consumer behaviour indicators include loyalty and penetration; consumer intermediate indicators include awareness and attitudes; input measures such as advertising's share of the marketing budget and competitive measures include share of market and voice and relative price. Its main innovation in the early 1990s was the use of 'traffic lights' to indicate improving, steady and worsening performance. Thus a complex chart covering these twenty-odd indicators for many countries (columns) instantly communicated overall performance to busy top management, which reviews one page for each of their top global brands. The colour dominance of red, green or amber says it all.

Unilever has a similar system. Both companies, after some internal difficulties, have standardized the measures across brands and countries. Diageo allows some differences between Burger King, spirit brands and Pillsbury's food products, but they are minor.

Companies adopt both formal and informal processes to get from 'many' to market-focused measures. Some gather senior marketers from different sectors and countries to trade their experiences of the various indicators and discuss how useful they are. As marketers are known for their strong opinions, the exchange can often be a marketing education in itself. Some form of external moderation is usually required. Alternatively or additionally, statistical tests can be run over years to see which metrics correlate with each other and with performance, which oscillate wildly and which barely move at all. This quickly shows which indicators are candidates for the chop.

For multinational companies, the decision to move from many measures to a more focused approach seems to be driven by corporate style. Multi-locals like Nestlé prefer diversity, while those seeking globalization, like Diageo and Unilever, push for consistency. They are more likely to have strong central market research (information) departments and to be seeking learning from country-to-country comparisons. These are difficult without harmonized metrics. In large companies, data warehouses can be maintained at lower diagnostic levels so that adjustments can be made without losing continuity.

This, however, is limited by whether data can be purchased. More sophisticated measures are available in the US but not in all countries worldwide. Even where available, collecting data on small brands in small countries may be too expensive. Flexibility has to be left for change and development. And determining the brand unit can be troublesome where there are complicated brand architectures. Where one brand name spans many product types, the unit will usually be the brand–product combination, but this can vary depending on country and product. For example, Sony video recorders in Brazil would be a single brand market unit. Performance for this may be quite different from Walkman in Brazil or Sony video recorders in Mexico.

All these pragmatic factors will determine the number of metrics suitable for each company. As a rule, larger companies can handle more, say twenty, metrics because they have more to draw on, whereas SMEs may need only five or six.

Stage five: scientific

Most top marketing companies aspire to the final stage but few have reached it. The problem is technical: few companies have a comprehensive database for all types of metrics, product groups and countries where the data is strictly comparable over many years. Where such a database is available, all the candidate measures can be subjected to quantitative analysis, to determine which are best for predicting future performance. The fact that certain past metrics predicted today's performance is not, of course, a guarantee that today's metrics will predict tomorrow's – but it helps. The resulting pool of metrics needs to be widened to allow for this uncertainty. From this widened pool, the best-performing metrics can be presented to top management. In other words, the database needs to hold a broader selection of measures than are used at any single point of time to allow evolution.

The scientific stage involves continuous modelling which can also be seen as developing an expert system. As results come through, they are compared with predictions and the model parameters adapt progressively. Of course, no computer system can predict discontinuous changes and those are precisely the ones that matter most. On the other hand they can identify discontinuous change more quickly (as unexplained variance) and they can systematize marketing performance assessment to improve managerial learning.

The reality is that this stage is an ideal. None of our respondents claimed to be there yet. We know the modelling tools exist and that specialist services, such as Novaction, provide both databases and techniques for forecasting. There may well be advanced use of these techniques for overall board-level reporting and users may be keeping quiet for commercial reasons. What does, of course, routinely exist is the use of such models for testing variations of marketing mix (communications, packaging, pricing, product enhancement and promotion). A small amount of empirical data can be enhanced to provide reliable estimates of national demand. These, however, are different applications from overall marketing performance assessment. Perhaps, for the wider remit, organizations just do not stay still long enough for the scientific callipers to be applied.

Nevertheless, the board should apply pressure to move the evolution of metrics to the scientific stage. Which senior director takes this responsibility is a matter of context, but for reasons set out in Chapter 7, the author's view is that it should usually be the finance director.

Balancing financial and non-financial measures at board level

The main message is that any meeting with financial reports, and that means every board meeting, should have some tracking of market indicators, albeit not many. We saw earlier how Bradford and Bingley track customer defection and retention rates monthly. Many other companies track customer satisfaction and, better, satisfaction *relative* to their key competitors. At the same time, no firm should conduct thorough marketing reviews more than quarterly and that is arguably too frequent. Too much routine destroys fresh insight.

For the main annual or semi-annual review, the full set is needed to be objective with as little room as possible for brand managers to manipulate the metrics to give a partial view. For example, forecasts are automatically suspect: the board is looking for the state of brand equity today and the marketing performance over the recent past. Year-to-year consistency, in terms of both which indicators are used and how they are compared, is important since it is the change, not the snapshot, that is important. For the same reason, indicators should not reflect only the current strategy, which changes periodically, but rather a representative range of strategies for all seasons. Because metrics need trends, they adjust to new strategy more slowly than a supertanker changes course.

Note that the set of metrics depends little on whether the company sees marketing as pan-company, departmental, in terms of expenditure or all three. The lower levels are *incremental* to pan-company efforts. Pan-company marketing is universal but not every company needs a specialist marketer or marketing department. As noted earlier, boards need to review specialist needs, just like any other specialist needs, periodically.

Thus once one gets below the pan-company marketing level, the specialist marketers share accountability for brand market unit performance but additionally have direct accountability for the tasks that are assigned to them. This includes the incremental cost benefits from the marketing expenditure.

Lloyds/TSB

The Lloyds/TSB business is divided into product marketing units such as savings and credit cards, each of which has its own marketing function in addition to the group function under Ford Ennals. The board reviews marketing metrics quarterly and advertising results monthly. A current priority is to measure effectiveness of marketing spend against sales and the levers that drive sales. 'Marketing' means what the specialist function does.

The group is one of the leaders in shareholder value-based management that has brought more focus on the customer. Consumer indicators are the priority, with the numbers of new customers gained and retained being key metrics. In the future the unit of analysis will shift from product groups to consumer target groups. Marketing assessment is at the 'financial' stage of evolution.

Source: Metrics interview with Alison Freund, Head of Research and Information, 3 December 1998.

Segmentation and alignment

Consistency requires that performance be compared with objectives and with competition for the same brand market segment, in order to compare like with like. Similarly, the BMS unit should be unchanged from year to year.

A typical example would be a product like Maybelline, a beauty product sold by L'Oréal, which markets many beauty brands globally. Maybelline in Taiwan would be a single BMS if all its end users were in the same segment (young females). However, if Maybelline were marketed separately to younger and older female users, perhaps with different products under the same brand, each would be a separate BMS.

Note in this context that segmentation is more than dividing end users into homogeneous clusters. As a rule of thumb each segment, and therefore BMS, needs its own manager and its own marketing plan and subsequent assessment. But this overhead puts a brake on the number of BMS units a firm, and especially a small firm, can handle.

So while segmentation has long been regarded as textbook best practice, its administrative complexity and cost inhibit implementation. Segmentation is more praised in theory than in execution. Mail-order firm Argos, for example, prefers to treat all customers together. Publisher EMAP, however, segments customers by 'attitude (streetwise, into cars, anti-establishment, inward/outward focused, attitude to subject matter) and (less importantly) age and social class.'[3]

Lifetime customer value, in theory if not in practice, has a major influence on whether formal segmentation is worthwhile, especially in financial services where service provision is targeted at the most profitable segments. Whether that is at the expense of the less profitable is a contentious issue for those who believe that bank accounts and low interest payments are entitlements for all. What matters here is the importance of aligning the firm's goals, market segments and metrics.

The Royal Mail, for example, has a database with 1.2 million business customer records. For their direct mail activities they can segment their markets by revenue and type of revenue, customer loyalty, sector, seniority of customer contact and many other dimensions.

Despite these examples of good practice, my view is that for most companies consumer segmentation is a good way to empathize with different consumer groups but is too complex for formal partition of plans, data and metrics. Only where separate management exists anyway (e.g. for shareholder relations) should 'customers' be segmented – e.g. as set out in Table 2.1. Thus the alignment needs to be strategic rather than detailed. As some of the difficulty arises from data collection, I will return to segmentation in Chapter 7.

Most companies cope with a single brand in one market with more or less homogeneous consumers. Nestlé, by contrast, with its 8,500 brands in 200 world markets, cannot monitor them all at board level. Multinational boards manage the difficulty by identifying the relatively few brand market units that make up most of the profit. By tracking individual as well as group totals, they can stay close to their sources of cash flow.

The findings presented below are consistent with Metrics research on strategic alignment and segmentation.

Aligning strategic performance measures and results

Strategic performance measurement (SPM) as a route to improved business results is a key issue for chief executives, according to a study carried out by the Conference Board, the global business research organization. It is based on advice and feedback from A T Kearney, chief financial officers, corporate strategists, a survey of 113 companies and a review of current business literature. Companies in the study include Siemens, Caterpillar, Dow Chemical and National Power.

Findings:

- 77% of the companies responding said that SPM is very important to the chief executive officer (CEO), and in half the companies the CEO leads the process.
- Companies whose share price outperforms that of their competitors are likely to have a formal SPM system. While the SPM system may be characterized primarily as either value-based management or Balanced Scorecard in origin, there is no statistically significant difference between them. Many companies attempt to integrate these two systems.
- Companies whose share price outperforms that of their competitors are likely to use an SPM system to communicate feedback about SPM targets to division and senior managers as well as to the board. SPM systems can gauge progress on strategic goals, which is a major advantage to management, and can also assist the board in making difficult divestment or restructuring decisions.
- In addition, companies whose share price outperforms that of their competitors are discussing SPM targets with investors and analysts, thereby opening a new channel of communication with those professionals who value strategic information highly.
- Over the next three years, a majority of companies expect to publish SPM targets and results in their annual reports. Additionally, over the next three years, the most frequently cited financial SPMs will be cash flow, return on capital employed, and economic profit. The most frequently cited non-financial SPMs are customer satisfaction, market share and new product development.
- An overwhelming majority of companies will link their SPM system to business unit strategy plans and incentive compensation over the next three years. The majority of companies are aligning performance measurements down to the business unit level and linking them with incentive compensation targets.

However, the study finds some major challenges facing companies trying to implement these systems. First, the systems are not viewed as 'strategic' enough and are focused on internal goals, such as tracking financial or operating activities, rather than on strategic goals.

Second, translating the vision and strategic objectives down to performance measures relevant to activities at the business unit level is proving difficult, as is getting 'buy-in' from business unit managers and employees.

Third, information technology capabilities are often deficient to support what the SPM systems demand. Finally, the cultural and political resistance can be strong, although only 9% of responding companies consider identifying key stakeholder reasons for resisting the SPM effort.

One major problem identified by the study is the fact that although chief financial officers and corporate strategists have to rely on the skills of other professionals to develop new measures for human resources activities like employee development and performance, or marketing measures for brands and customer satisfaction, not one respondent mentioned HR or marketing professionals as participants in the development or maintenance of SPMs.

Source: *Aligning Strategic Performance Measures and Results*, Report No. 1261-99-RR, the Conference Board, 1999.

In large companies the alignment of strategy and measurement needs sustained task force activity. The whole firm needs to evolve through the stages. The task force needs to assess the workshops, costs and timetable that will be needed. Metrics need to be fully integrated with the rest of the data warehouse: they are simply the part of the iceberg visible to the board. A separate stand-alone metrics system may provide a quick fix but will surely fail as the dislocation from the main stream cuts off routine data supply.

Organizations can be profoundly affected by this process, not structurally but culturally. The adoption of a shared market orientation should change the way functions work together, the data they get and the data they share.

The challenge to the task force is to design a programme that will move smoothly from the present stage toward the scientific, without disruption, while taking the rest of the team with them. They have asked not to be named but one of the best-known, and most successful, consumer packaged goods companies in the world embarked on this path only in 1999. They represent best practice, but best practice is not out of reach.

Executive minutes 4

1 Assess the current and required stage of metrics evolution.

2 Have the task force report on workshops for all management, costs and timetable.

3 Board agendas to include monthly and annual or semi-annual marketing metrics cycles. Marketing to recommend just a few key market indicators to balance monthly financials. The periodic full review to include the year-on-year change in brand equity.

4 Marketing performance to be assessed top-down, i.e. pan-company first, before consideration of the incremental contribution by specialist marketers and budgets.

5 Finance and marketing directors to identify jointly the priority brand market units for board review individually, based on proportion of shareholder value. Other units to be reported in aggregate.

6 Align goals, plans and measurement as closely as possible. Where they change from year to year, double-run the metrics to preserve comparative figures.

References

1   CIA MediaLab *Finance Directors Survey 2000*. Research conducted by NOP Corporate and Financial. Published by IPA in association with KPMG and the *Financial Times*, 14 February 2000.

2   Meyer, Marshall W. (1998) 'Measuring and managing performance: the new discipline in management', Neely, Andy D. and Waggoner, Daniel B., eds., in *Performance Measurement: Theory and Practice*, vol. 1, Cambridge: Judge Institute, xiv–xxi.

3   'The Role of Marketing', KPMG Research Report 1999, 6.

Measuring innovation health

This chapter signals a change of gear. We move from the overview of metrics evolution to the most difficult area for measurement: innovation. So far, we have been looking more to the external market and excluded innovation and internal marketing (employees) from consideration. Most respondents did this too, but when reminded about innovations and the crucial role of employees (which is covered in the next chapter) they agreed that the topic needed to be broadened in those ways. Nearly all our respondents rated innovation as a top priority, but also one in which their assessment systems fell short.

The chapter is concerned with any kind of innovation that may affect market performance. Marketers told us that their attention had switched from ever smaller product variations to new ways of delivering customer satisfaction. Producing yet another flavour of potato snacks was merely boring the consumer. Our respondents were seeking greater innovation, and yet most of their firms suffered from innovation, or perhaps initiative, overload. Quantity too often damages quality.

Figure 5.1 gives an overview of this chapter, which addresses these issues:

- Identifying the drivers, enablers and moderators of innovation. Counting innovations is less useful than measuring the strategic, cultural and process indicators of a firm's innovation health.

- Agreeing the menu. The board needs to resolve a few issues before metrics can be established. Issue 1 is that the board should seek to avoid choosing

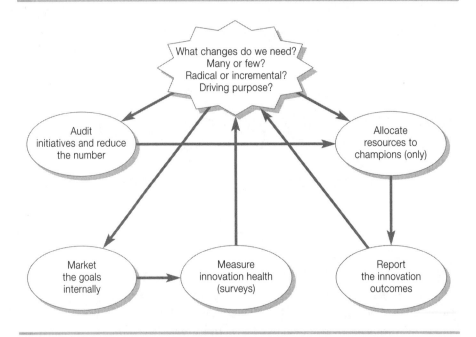

Fig 5.1 ■ Innovation health metrics

between innovations. Instead they need to create the climate in which the right number and types of innovation can blossom.

■ Devising a short list of innovation health metrics.

The first section models how innovation happens. Culture and process are not drivers so much as enablers or, more often, disablers. The right culture and process will not guarantee innovation but when they are wrong, innovation will be blocked. We then review strategy, culture and process in more detail before reverting to the context that the board needs to set. The last section presents a short list of innovation metrics, which was evolved from the much longer list that forms Appendix C. Finally, as shown by Figure 5.1, implementation comes to the fore.

The main conclusion drawn from the Metrics research was that top management should be less directly concerned with innovations. They should agree the menu and then get out of the kitchen. When the corporate purpose and zest for marketplace action collide with organizational knowledge, great innovation can result. We have encountered this double negative – of marketers avoiding what not to do – before, and it sets up a neat paradox: knowledge is the enemy of learning.

Large and successful companies have the advantage of knowing more than their lesser competitors. It is not just a matter of scale: Procter and Gamble, 3M and Wal-Mart have developed processes that work, and sharpened their ability to sense alternatives that do not fit their patterns and reject them. Their organizational knowledge comes from experience, intuition, consumer empathy and market research. Learning, however, gives rise to zest that can prove this organizational knowledge wrong. The difficulty lies in finding the balance. Innovation must be focused; it cannot challenge, still less change, everything all of the time. So innovation will be characterized as naïve enthusiasm wresting a solution from harsh reality.

We all recognize that both extremes – of excessive innovation and none at all – are sub-optimal. The question is how measurement can help direct the business towards the right amount and types of innovation; in other words, towards 'innovation health'.

The concern with monitoring innovation health is not universal. Amongst those we talked to, the outstanding innovators create so naturally that they were amazed by our questions. To them, innovation health is the oxygen in the air: you breathe it, not measure it. At the other extreme, the stick-in-the-muds, sometimes those who now hold the power, see change as a threat. They will not consider innovation, still less measure it. This chapter, then, is addressed to those who want innovation to improve per-formance and to use measurement as part of that.

Innovation permeates so much of business that we need to be clear about the unit of analysis for marketing metrics. We are not considering every kind of innovation – just the things that affect the market. The list below defines the subject of this chapter.

What we are concerned with

Innovation The creation, development and implementation of goods, services, service delivery and any new activity that will affect the firm's performance in the market. Thus we are not just concerned with product innovation. Purely internal innovation, though important, is excluded for marketing metrics purposes.

Performance Profits and growth resulting from innovation. In other words, we are looking at *successful* innovations not just launches that may fail.

Innovation health The fitness in all these three areas – creativity, development and implementation – which in turn deliver innovation performance. Some businesses are good at only one or two.

Management control While many environmental or emergent factors affect innovation performance, we are concerned with practical metrics that a board can use for decision-making and monitoring.

Innovation in general, not just any single one The factors that may cause a single particular innovation to succeed (e.g. massacring all other innovations) may not be good for the business unit as a whole.

Strategic business unit While we are primarily concerned with the whole firm, reality is that each business unit may have different kinds of leadership and culture. These key details can be lost in aggregation. At the same time, we are not addressing innovation at the level of the individual or team or brand market segment.

Both radical and incremental Conditions for creating sector-changing, discontinuous innovation may be quite different from, perhaps in conflict with, conditions for many small incremental (i.e. *kaizen*) changes.

Drivers, enablers and moderators of innovation

Innovation is under the spotlight. John Kearon, a founding partner in Brand Genetics, one of the UK's leading innovation agencies, claims that 'large companies no longer have the ability to originate the sort of new category brands that made them successful in the first place.'[1] Others have similarly concluded that innovation processes in large companies stifle the radical developments that the firms seek.

Yet there are more product launches, new media, new advertising and promotion campaigns than ever before. The profusion of marketing offerings is expanding faster than consumers can absorb them. In the 1990s, probably more new organizational processes were invented each year than in any past century. Initiative overload in large companies, fuelled to some extent by empowerment, creates constipation. The net result is less innovation, not more. Yet change in the world is widely perceived as accelerating. Maybe it is, or this perception may be merely a symptom of age. All we know for sure is that we need to get better in a hurry.

The sort of innovation we most want is the kind that gives marketplace advantage, which in turn puts a generous dollop on the bottom line. We would all like to be able to distinguish, early on, the winning initiatives from the duds. Unfortunately, although very sophisticated analysis can help spot *certain* losers, measurement can do little to identify winners. The telephone, the Beatles, Baileys Irish Cream and many, many other great innovations were derided early on. In this chapter, therefore, we focus on measuring the innovation health *of a business as a whole*, not proposing a system to test individual innovations.

So if we cannot identify winners early on, what do we measure? We have found no companies that are confident they have the answers. The most popular metric, led by 3M, is the proportion of sales represented by products launched in the last three or five years. But this measure looks back, not forward: companies need to know how they stand today – and particularly what can be changed today to improve performance tomorrow. At the same time, past successes are a valuable indication of continuing health.

Debating innovation at the London Business School faculty lunch table showed that we each approach innovation with our own habitual way of thinking. As a marketer, I know the issue is market-driven, but colleagues in strategy, organizational behaviour and logistics assured me it was all a matter of strategy, culture and supply chain processes respectively. Had I consulted financial, R&D and IT colleagues, shareholder value, R&D and information would have been identified as the drivers. A year of dispute provided Figure 5.2, which brings the key components together. Innovation cannot be understood in isolation but as an output from a well-functioning firm. A tree puts out a new branch because it is healthy. A botanist can go round counting branches (innovations) but will learn very little. Understand why the tree is healthy and branch-making falls into place. Transplanting 3M's metrics into a firm without similar strategy, culture and processes will be a waste of time.

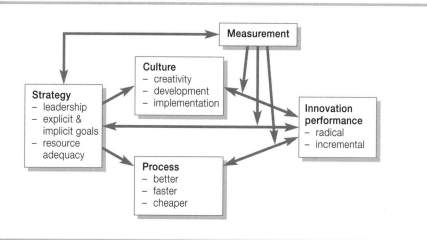

Fig 5.2 ■ Drivers, enablers and moderators of innovation performance

Thus, in Figure 5.2 strategy is the primary *driver* of innovation whereas culture and processes are the *enablers*. In other words, culture and processes will not *cause* innovation to happen but, if they are wrong, innovation will fail. In practice serendipity strikes and change comes about in all manner of ways, but purposive innovation requires CEOs to define, for starters, how much, and what type of, innovation they need. Strategy is the cornerstone, but CEOs cannot be expected to be too specific as to exactly what innovation they expect. On the other hand, they can, and should, indicate the direction and scale of innovation.

Meanwhile, compare Figure 5.2 with the Arthur D. Little framework reproduced here as Table 5.1.[2] This, too, sees the key components as strategy, process and culture. The definition of strategy in the next section includes resources. For each of these they suggest metrics that may lag, lead or be contemporary (real time) with events and may also monitor the learning from these events. This leads them to eight metrics as in the table.

Table 5.1 ■ The Arthur D. Little innovation metrics framework and representative metrics

	Lagging	Real time	Leading	Learning
Stakeholder strategies	Gross contribution of new products	NPV of idea portfolio		
Processes		Milestones completed on time		Take-up rate of new processes
Resources			External alliances being pursued	
Culture/ organization	Staff turnover rate		Innovation climate	Level of inquiry

This table shows the importance of learning from all stages of the dynamic processes involved in innovation.

Strategy

For some writers the word 'strategy' means whatever they want it to mean.[3] Etymologically, its derivation is 'what generals do', and that is just three things: they provide leadership, goals and adequate resourcing (people and money). Tactics (the battle plan) are consequential to strategy.

A general does most of these three *before* the battle, although the plan, for example, may alter in the light of changing circumstances. Nevertheless the reality is that business, unlike warfare, is conducted with plans that are implicit as much as explicit and, unlike a battle, business cycles have no clear beginning and end. For convenience we chop time into annual pieces. In the annual plan, the financial figures are clear enough but purpose, direction and goals are often implicit. Managers do not write down what everyone already knows. What is certain is that, however informal, *some* sense of direction and purpose is essential. Strategy writer Gary Hamel calls it 'strategic intent'.[4] In this view, formal planning gives way to an empowered workforce that is aware of direction. To head west in sunlight you need only the time of day, not a detailed map.

Strategy in this model therefore has three measurable components: leadership, goals and resource adequacy. Goals need to be defined with sufficient clarity to drive, and to be compared with, performance, but not be so detailed as to inhibit opportunism. Our research indicated very clear financial goals but less specificity about non-financial innovation goals.

Leadership primarily entails the motivation of the business unit to achieve those goals. Awareness is not enough: commitment needs to be researched too. Metrics can play a key role in communicating and securing commitment to goals, e.g. the Balanced Scorecard. Managers need to be aware of what *kinds* of innovation are required. Which brand market segment units need most innovation? What should be the balance between continuous small improvements (*kaizen*) and radical innovation?

Many different leadership styles have proved effective. The search for a one-fits-all has been unproductive and is probably foolish. The context of the market, the competitive environment and corporate culture determine what type of leadership is appropriate. Elaine Underwood supplied her own variety at J A Sharwood.

J A Sharwood & Co

J A Sharwood & Co is part of the £3.6 billion Tomkins group. Turnover exceeds £60 million in a range of branded ethnic chutneys and sauces. At the time of the interview, Elaine Underwood had been Managing Director since 1994.

One way Sharwood's encourages fresh thinking is to send combined marketing and product development teams out to stay in the markets themselves such as southern India, Singapore or China to see what people actually eat, not what is being cooked in swanky restaurants. According to Underwood, this has brought about an enormous improvement in innovation: the team works together on project management with commitment and passion as a result of having been out there originating the ideas in those countries. She thinks that the promotion of innovation is giving people the chance to do things as if they were sitting around with a clean sheet of paper.

She believes that the most difficult job is the internal communication of business strategy. She is constantly finding new ways to get it across in 'quick, easy ways to remember'. Complex mission and value statements and detailed objectives are too difficult, so strategy is simplified for communication.

The parent group has a strong financial orientation. In response marketing has developed its own version of the Balanced Scorecard with a range of indicators of marketing effectiveness. A monthly innovation report card shows turnover from products in their first two years in the market. Sharwood is developing an activity-based costing system to get away from allocations and to understand real costs. New processes and better estimates of product and customer profitability should result.

Tying up financial performance with management rewards has some way to go but what is clear is the importance of 'clear objectives and then being given the skills and tools to achieve them'.

Source: Laura Mazur interview with Elaine Underwood, November 1998.

No company has all the resources for the innovation it could undertake and allocation is part of the process consideration below. At the same time, there must be some broad sense that there is enough slack in the treasury and human resources to invest in the future. A firm that talks long-term but routinely axes projects without short-term payback will soon run short of strategic initiatives. In measurement terms, it may be enough to ask for managers' perceptions of resource adequacy. If those expected to achieve the goals think there is enough, there probably is. On the other hand, the perception of inadequate resources may be due to poor communications, reluctance to innovate, or 'not invented here'. Alternatively, they may be right. Positive managers will use reduced resources against a narrower target, whereas others will use this to justify inaction. But then Field Marshal Montgomery was right not to attack a better general at Alamein until he had superior resources.

In summary, strategy metrics are the innovation goals themselves, staff awareness and commitment to those goals, and staff acceptance that adequate resources are available. Goals need to be quantified so that performance can be benchmarked against them. What about the *type* of innovation required (radical versus *kaizen*) and how tightly will efforts be focused? The former should be supplied by the corporate and innovation goals. Vague pieties about increasing size or share, even if quantified, will not motivate the troops. Strategy means expressing, in broad terms, *how* those business objectives will be realized. At the very least, the strategy should say whether the firm will do what it now does better and/or attempt something new.

Similarly, focus is the flip side of resource adequacy. The fewer resources available, the tighter the focus will need to be. That is easy to say, but not so easy to measure. Simply asking managers up to their fetlocks in crocodiles whether the drainage is adequate may not provide valuable data. Nevertheless, in concluding with resource adequacy as a key metric, and recognizing measurement difficulty, the intention is to represent both sides of the coin.

Culture

Culture has an enabling, or disabling, effect on all three stages of innovation: creativity, development and implementation. Obviously the culture itself does not change at each stage: the stages themselves are different and make separate demands on the way the firm operates. Creativity may get the most attention but the more prosaic business of converting the idea to reality and market launch are just as crucial. The *mechanics* of all three are perhaps process rather than culture, but the mechanics turn out to matter less than the climate within which they operate. Nevertheless, we should begin with creativity. Professor Teresa Amabile and her colleagues at Harvard have developed one of the best models thus far of corporate culture and creativity (Figure 5.3).[5]

In this view, creativity is a sensitive flower that needs to be encouraged at organizational, immediate supervisory and peer group levels. Like autonomy and resource adequacy, this encouragement has a positive effect on creativity. As we move down the left side of the chart, the picture becomes more mixed. Challenging work has a positive motivational effect but not if it is excessive. Too many pressures, organizational blockages or approval hurdles become negative, shown in Figure 5.3 as '–ve'. All the factors in this model are positive except workload pressures and organizational impediments.

These and similar models have been tested and represent some degree of consensus both in academia and with our practitioner discussants. Key performance indicators, and measurement in general, were seen as examples of organizational impediments and thereby negative. Joseph Bonner and colleagues looked at management control of product development and concluded that 'less appears to be better'.[6] Cross-functional teams should be given considerable autonomy to devise their own targets, within broad

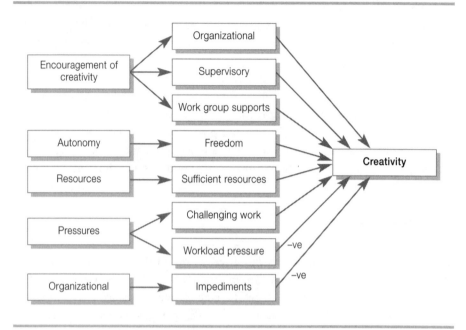

Fig 5.3 ■ Amabile et al. Conceptual Model (KEYS)

strategic direction, as well as processes and procedures. Their findings applied to both incremental and radical innovation.

This picture may be too utopian. As noted at the beginning of the chapter, no company can grant freedom to all managers to be creative and change everything all of the time. Something somewhere has to apply the firm's existing knowledge and disciplines to achieve focus. So whilst sympathizing with Bonner's 'less' process is better, the culture must include opposition. Innovation is unlikely to succeed in the external marketplace if it has not been thoroughly tested in the internal one first.

Part of the answer lies in the cross-functional nature of innovation teams. Divergent perspectives within the team should hammer the innovation into shape before it sees even internal light of day. In particular, one or more team members need to play the part of the recalcitrant customer.

In industrial markets customers supply and even drive their suppliers' innovations. So do retailers for their own brands (private label). Mary Sonnack, Division Scientist at 3M, has worked with innovation expert MIT's Professor Eric von Hippel, using his depth interviews of 'users in the extreme'.[7] As with consumer research, 'routine users' cannot imagine what innovations they will like. Superficial research will only reveal the obvious, which, in turn, is most likely to fail. Hippel and other top innovators get much deeper into understanding the problems the firm's, and competitors', products now solve and how they might be improved. Furthermore, innovation now deals with the way the goods and services are delivered, to make end use easier and/or more enjoyable.

All the positive parts of the Amabile model (learning) need to be challenged by the harsh-reality side of culture (knowledge). The innovation teams need to be experienced in all parts of the business. Do not put the new kid on the block in charge of innovation. The more that organizational knowledge can be applied *within* the team, the less friction will have to be applied when it gets into the wider internal market. But the harsh side can be expressed positively: knowledge can be enforced or it can be actively sought by team members. They can 'learn voraciously', as Dell puts it. Assimilated knowledge means someone else never having to say 'no'.

Dell

Michael Dell attributes much of his success to well-hired people all of whom have a sense of personal investment. He provides eight tips:

- Learn voraciously
- Teach innovative thinking
- Encourage smart experimentation
- Beware the perils of pride
- Do not try to perfume a pig
- Communicate fast and deeply
- Stay allergic to hierarchy
- Mobilize people around a single goal.

Together these amount to responsibility, accountability and shared success but people have to feel it is safe to fail. Giving them the knowledge and permission to do what they do best, ensuring that staff see themselves as owners, brings more success to a company, according to Dell, than anything else he has found.

Source: Dell, Michael (1999) *Direct from Dell: Strategies that Revolutionized an Industry*. Harper Collins.

Creativity is only the first part of the story. Innovation performance requires creativity *and* effective development skills *and* good implementation to deliver the innovations. These cultural characteristics may be in conflict: the freedom to create may not fit well with the discipline required to deliver.

One solution to this is to separate these roles, by, for example, giving the role of creating initiatives to one task force, or outsourcing it, and giving development and implementation to others. This has the superficial advantage of specialization but experience does not support it. New concepts are not neat parcels that can be passed from group to group, but ill-defined, unwrapped intuitions, which a team can hold and believe in passionately but which will fall apart when they are passed to unbelievers. GrandMet's portfolio of adult soft drinks (Dexter's, Aqua Libra and Purdey's) pioneered the category but lost its way with changes of management.

Our research has found overwhelming support for cross-functional teams with high levels of autonomy to see the whole project through. As well as enabling all functional issues to be considered ahead of time, it is likely that the high cost and administrative drag of these teams, especially full-time teams, forces top management to prioritize initiatives. The Fluke corporation provides an example of how team-centred innovation can be set loose.

The Phoenix process at Fluke Corporation

The Fluke Corporation has a $500 million turnover in compact professional electronic test tools such as handheld multimeters. In 1992, their peace dividend was negative: most of their business was tied up with the military. Phoenix was the name for the new process that started with a blank board. Joe Martins, Fluke's Business Development Manager, sees creativity as only a catalyst: a small amount of substance that speeds things up but is not consumed in the process. Other key ingredients are the commitment and enthusiasm of the teams that were initially made up of volunteers with little to lose – not the high-flyers.

Practical team details included two weeks to form a group of four to eight people, full-time, with a team manager, rules and analysis style, interaction with the rest of the organization and a project plan/milestones/reporting. Martins sees team identity as important. Each had a name, a mascot, rituals and a war room. They brought their hobbies into the process.

Rather than building a strong team spirit that might get in the way of adopting ideas from outside, they looked for affiliative characteristics, i.e. how people got along.

The de-emphasis above on creativity should not be taken literally. Fluke ran creativity training sessions and whenever minds got 'locked up' introduced 'crazy discussions about why the sky is blue or why is the grass green'.

Using the Phoenix process, four innovations, including two acquisitions, will soon account for about half of Fluke's turnover.

Source: Martins, Joe (1999) 'The Phoenix Process at Fluke Corporation', *Business Strategy Review* 10(1), 39–56.

Research into culture, innovation, organizational learning and knowledge is immense. The number of possible metrics is likewise too extensive for our purposes.[8] The three key enabling factors that emerge from the above culture summary are: freedom to fail, autonomy for the innovation team and a willingness to change by the firm as a whole. These need to be balanced by the application of knowledge. The friction, or interaction, between the encouraging and harsh sides of culture provide the spark for effective innovation. Put positively, it can be expressed as the appetite for learning. The freedom to fail comes with a responsibility to exhaust what the firm has already learned.

These four metrics can be reduced to a balance of two: freedom to fail and responsible knowledge, i.e. appetite for learning.

Process

In reviewing the different processes firms use to nurture or destroy innovation, we are looking for factors that excite the few successful Big Ideas, not the myriad initiatives that get in the way. Procter & Gamble found that the big winners were conceived and championed by a small number of key executives who were distinguished by their energy and a very high bandwidth of interests. Such creativity seems to be associated with 'outsights' (the opposite of tunnel vision), which are the peripheral associations most of us do not make.

3M, where the champion concept was born, supplies many examples of its importance. Champions are motivated by passion, not financial rewards, and a 'maverick' on the main board champions the champions. The successful champion is funded to travel the world to spread the gospel. In the alcoholic beverage industry, Baileys Irish Cream and canned draught Guinness are two other examples of successful use of the champion concept. The board may not be able, or wise, to measure the ROI of their creative ideas; but it can measure the number of true champions, defined as people who do not clear hurdles so much as crash through them. Approval hurdles are important for ensuring creative leaps matter too.

Novartis

Novartis was created by the merger of the Ciba Geigy and Sandoz groups in 1996 and covers healthcare products (60% of turnover), nutrition (Gerber), medical and food supplements and agribusiness. Professor Walter von Wartburg is Head of Communications.

Perhaps its biggest challenge has been to rise above its long history and take 100,000 people through a radical culture change to become an organization that is flexible and fast moving. 'You have to find the right balance between empowerment and control,' von Wartburg says. 'On the one hand you have to let loose, but on the other you have to have a tight rein. But where do you let loose and where do you have a tight rein? That is basically the art of management.'

A formal programme identifies and nurtures the next generation of managers and recruitment brings in bright young people even though there is no obvious career path. Novartis also spots the best research talent through a programme of prizes and recognition, where the three most innovative people are selected from the five- to six-thousand-strong research community.

Measurement covers both hard and soft areas. The hard include the number of products going from stage to stage and number of new patents, registrations and market launches. Soft measures deal with the way employees achieve results and whether behaviour matches the firm's core values.

Source: Laura Mazur interview with Professor von Wartburg, November 1998.

Professor Chris Voss, of London Business School, has reduced process characteristics to three groups: better, faster and cheaper.[9] Detailed examples are listed in Appendix C but we found that they did not feature on our respondents' short lists of the key innovation health metrics. Before bringing the final list together, it is worth itemizing some key issues the board should address.

Agreeing the menu

There is a very simple reason why the boards of large companies should seek to avoid active engagement in innovations. They have to be presumed to be the most knowledgeable members of the company and, as such, the most resistant to learning. So what should they be doing to foster and measure innovation health? Obviously the treatment depends on the firm's symptoms, but these are some general agenda items:

- Is a major audit required? If the status quo is a long way from the desired state, a full-scale investigation of strategy, culture and process issues may be needed, involving the sampling of a much broader range of measures than the handful of metrics recommended here for regular monitoring.

- Removing obvious disablers. Taking positive action to improve innovation is much more difficult than finding and removing the most visible obstructions. Junior managers will know what they are – probably process.

- Creating or revising the corporate goals and, within those, the specific goals for innovation. At the least they must show whether the intention is more and better of the same and/or radical change, and, if so, in what direction? The board needs to review the current level of innovation and take a view on quantity and quality.

- What will success look like? Setting the benchmarks against which performance will be measured.

- Instigating a major internal communication programme to achieve awareness and commitment to goals and benchmarks.

- Taking control of corporate initiatives. Generally, large firms have too many initiatives in play at any point in time. Each seems important, even a priority, when it is set up but few firms co-ordinate them in aggregate. This chapter is only concerned with market-oriented initiatives but the board may prefer a single system for all cross-functional initiatives. Some firms will wish to authorize such initiatives at board level; others will be more permissive. The recommendation here is merely that there is some annual census, the champion for each one is identified and, if there is no champion, the initiative is terminated. Even in a permissive company, the initiatives in process need to be compared with the goals and benchmarks. The balance is perhaps best indicated by failures, rather than successes. Are enough innovations getting through process for some to fail or are there too many failures? In the learning vs. knowledge head-to-head, which is getting the upper hand?

In terms of removing disablers, several practitioners singled out measurement, and KPIs in particular, for criticism. Too many indicators are chosen because they are easy to measure rather than because they give vital signs of innovation health. A simple exercise is to put oneself in the shoes of a new CEO walking into his new company one morning with no prior knowledge. What vital signs would indicate the company's innovation health? Combining those with the nine in the next section, then comparing them with the innovation-related measures the company now uses, should highlight the irrelevant and the counterproductive.

For example, a number of practitioners expect to find people in an innovative company having fun working there. The people in the Fluke

Corporation were clearly having fun. This may not be easy to measure, but KPIs such as expense reduction and time reporting are unlikely to help. Mechanistic as distinct from passionate processes, and differentiation for its own sake as distinct from offering something better, were similar targets for removal. 'Fun working here' was entertained as a metric but it did not make the short list. Nevertheless, look for the KPIs and other measures that are getting in the way and get rid of them.

A short list of innovation health metrics

Innovation is only part of the manageable list of marketing metrics for regular board review. If we only need five to describe brand equity, what is appropriate for innovation health? Table 5.2 provides nine, which was as far as I could condense them. Some companies will be able to go further. The long list of metrics we used to stimulate these responses is given in Appendix B.

The strategy and culture metrics are simply brought forward from the sections above. As we noted there, process is important but was not rated by our respondents as a regular metric. In place of that, the census of initiatives above provides the board with an overview of innovation process; and that is driven by the number of initiatives (shown as one of the outcome metrics). Similarly, the number of innovations getting through process into the marketplace, which can also be expressed as a percentage of those in process, provides some indication of productivity, albeit not directly supplying data on 'better/faster/cheaper'.

The list concludes with the most popular innovation metric: the share of sales revenue due to recent innovations.

Table 5.2 ■ Innovation metrics short list

Strategy	Awareness of goals (vision)
	Commitment to goals (vision)
	Active innovation support
	Resource adequacy
Culture	Appetite for learning
	Freedom to fail
Outcomes	No. of initiatives in process
	No. of innovations launched
	% revenue due to launches during last three years

Awareness of and commitment to innovation goals can be measured directly from staff surveys, as can the general question 'Are resources adequate for these goals?' On the other hand, they can also be seen as summary or index metrics built up from a greater number of more detailed questions, e.g. adequacy of finances for particular innovations.

The selected metrics take us back to creativity, development and implementation, each of which makes different demands on management. If we had a satisfactory metric for creativity *per se*, it would have been included. As it is, we can measure only the climate in which it *could* grow. For development and implementation too, culture and process are, after all, only enablers. The wish to learn is an indicator of high-bandwidth people likely to be innovators, and the freedom to fail also represents all kinds of autonomy. A higher-level 'innovation freedom' metric constructed from several indicators would be an alternative.

These nine metrics are simply a starting point for developing what is most relevant for your firm.

Executive minutes 5

1   If board is not satisfied with general state of innovation health, a full audit of strategy, culture, process, outcomes and internal communication should be authorized. This will need closer to ninety than the nine metrics suggested here for regular use.

2   Use the audit to weed out disabling factors – probably processes.

3   Re-establish corporate and innovation goals, metrics (adapted from the nine above) and performance benchmarks.

4   Ensure vigorous two-way international communication programme is in place to achieve awareness, commitment and an effective balance between resources and focus.

5   Review all initiatives in progress with champions. Cull those where enthusiasm is waning or reinvigorate them, perhaps with new champions.

6   Ensure major innovations have cross-functional teams who can balance zest for learning with harsh experience before initiatives are exposed to similar tests in the wider company, where they will still have to compete for resources to gain approval for launch.

7   Finance director to report metrics to board once or twice per annum, in addition to any individual applications for resources. Metrics to be compared with benchmarks, prior year and competitor information, as far as possible.

References

1   (1999) 'Innovation at a crossroads', *Market Leader* 6 (Autumn), 32–37, 32.

2   Collins, John and Smith, Darren (1999) 'Innovation metrics: a framework to accelerate growth', *Prism*, 1st Quarter, 33–47.

3   See 'In search of strategy' *Sloan Management Review* special issue 40 (3 Spring), 1999.

4   Hamel, Gary and Prahalad, C.K. (1994) 'Seeing the future first', *Fortune* (5 September), 64–8.

5   For example, Amabile, T.M.; Conti, R.; Coon, H.; Lazenby, J. and Herron, M. (1996) 'Assessing the work environment for creativity', *Academy of Management Journal* 39 (5), 1154–84.

6   Bonner, Joseph; Ruerkert, Robert W. and Walker, Orville C., Jr. (1998) 'Management control of product development projects', Cambridge, Mass.: Marketing Science Institute report 98–120, summary page.

7   *Marketplace*, Institute for the Study of Business Markets, Fall 1998, Penn State, 1.

8   For example, 24 factors are listed in DiBella, Anthony J. and Nevis, Edwin C. (1998) *How Organizations Learn*, San Francisco: Jossey-Bass.

9   Voss, C.A.; Johnston, R.; Silvestro, R.; Fitzgerald, L. and Brignall, T.J. (1992) 'Measurement of innovation and design performance in services', *Design Management Journal* (winter), 40–6.

6

Internal marketing metrics

A firm's first customers are its own employees. If the staff understand and wholeheartedly endorse the firm's marketing goals, they will take care of the external customers. BP Amoco, for example, market-researches its own managers as a proxy for external research. What is in the employees' heads can be called 'employer brand equity'.[1] Nothing will be gained by debating whether external marketing is more important than internal, and vice versa: what is certain is that internal marketing matters, and should precede external efforts.

With this in mind, the lessons of previous chapters still apply: the 'customer segment' becomes the employees and the brand is the corporate, or employer, brand. Employer brand equity needs to be motivated and maximized. Sensible measurement can help monitor progress against both historic and competitor benchmarks. Various metrics will be reviewed, and this will lead to the conclusion that innovation health and employer brand metrics are so similar that they can be merged.

Figure 6.1 provides an overview of the chapter, which is organized into these sections:

- The case for employee 'buy-in'. This introduces one approach to measuring employer brand equity;

- The link between company performance and employee attitudes;

- Employer brand measurement in a single-brand, single-business-unit company;

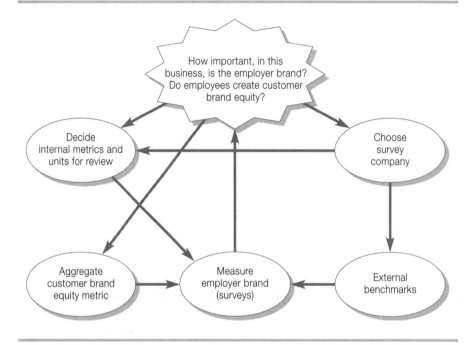

Fig 6.1 ■ Internal marketing metrics

- The complexities of a multi-brand business;

- Whether business units in a large group can be consolidated, i.e. whether the board should review a single set of employer brand metrics for the whole organization. Averages are very likely to be grey rather than black or white. Metrics need to be informative, and board presentation needs to highlight areas of success and those in need of improvement.

First, we need to note an important difference: for the external market the unit of analysis is the brand market segment, but for innovation health and for the employer brand the business unit applies. In a complex organization with a portfolio of brands and a variety of trading names, the 'brand', so far as individual employees are concerned, may vary across the organization. For simplicity here, I assume a single employing entity, although, in the last section, multiple consumer brands are allowed, e.g. as for Unilever.

The case for employee 'buy-in'

Strategic marketing consultancy Marketing & Communications Agency (MCA)[2] has been specializing in helping companies to align staff with business goals for a number of years. MCA proposes that only two indicators are needed to assess employee 'buy-in': understanding of, and commitment to, the company's business goals and brand values. Buy-in has two aspects: intellectually staff need to be aware of, and aligned with, key business strategies and what difference they can make. The other, equally valuable, side of the coin is the need for commitment and engagement in the achievement of goals. Emotion (passion) fuels an organization like gasoline fuels a car.

To understand the components and value of buy-in, MCA commissioned Market & Opinion Research International (MORI) to conduct a nationally representative quota sample of 350 managers and staff from British organizations employing 1,000 or more people within a cross-section of industry sectors.[3] About 60% worked in organizations with 5,000+ employees, and 41% were managers.

The survey was undertaken to gauge the levels of staff understanding of and commitment to their organizations' business objectives and goals – on both emotional and intellectual levels.

Interviews were carried out in respondents' homes using CAPI (Computer Assisted Personal Interviewing). Data has been weighted to reflect the national population profile. Where responses do not add up to 100%, the balance is accounted for by those who neither agree nor disagree or those who don't know, or is due to the rounding of figures.

To compare the levels of intellectual and emotional buy-in and to understand the areas for improvement, respondents were asked about their level of agreement with key benchmarking statements based on MCA's work with some of *The Times*' 100 companies. The results are summarized as Table 6.1.

Only 14% strongly agree with all five intellectual benchmarking statements. When asked about overall awareness and understanding of key business goals, less than half (48%) of respondents rate them as high.

On the emotional side, 51% of respondents rated their overall level of commitment as high. Nonetheless, the responses to the emotional benchmarking statements show a noticeable drop in levels of agreement overall: for example, Table 6.1 shows that only 9% of those interviewed felt their views and participation were valued by their organization. And only 15% strongly

Table 6.1 ■ Indicators of buy-in

(Note: Intellectual indicators are in *italics* and emotional in plain text.)	Strongly agree
I understand what I need to do in my own job to support organizational aims and goals	39%
I feel I play an important part in meeting our customers' needs	38%
I have the knowledge/skills to do my job in a way that supports organizational goals	37%
I can see how my job performance affects my organization's success	34%
The people in my team/work area know how we contribute to organizational goals	28%
I have a clear sense of my organization's vision and direction for the future	27%
I am committed to giving my best to help my organization succeed	27%
My organization's culture encourages me to work in innovative ways	17%
I believe in my organization's vision for the future	16%
I have confidence in my organization's leadership	15%
My views and participation are valued by my organization	9%

agreed that they have confidence in their organization's leadership. Only 5% of the respondents strongly agreed with all six emotional benchmarks.

Managers are being hit more heavily by change, which may explain their disappointing levels of understanding and commitment. About 40% say a restructuring or merger/acquisition has directly affected them in the last 12 months, compared with 29% of non-managers.

Levels of communication and internal marketing during periods of dramatic organizational change can have profound effects on the overall effectiveness of staff. An example is provided by two Fortune 500 companies that merged in the 1980s.[4] One plant received no communication until the formal announcement; the other had received early and frequent communication throughout the planning process. The plant without communication saw a 20% decrease in performance, a 24% increase in uncertainty, a 21% decrease in job satisfaction and an 11% decrease in commitment. The plant with early and frequent communication saw no change in performance or commitment and only a 2% decrease in job satisfaction.

According to MCA, the combination of intellectual and emotional buy-in creates people who are both willing and able to give their best to help their organization achieve its vision and goals, and who will act as ambassadors for their brand and/or organization.

These champions are vital to overcoming the neutral or negative responses likely from others in their organization. This is, of course, a different use of the word 'champion' from the one in the previous chapter, although a champion in this sense is more likely to be a successful leader of an innovation. Perspectives, the MORI normative database, found that about one in five UK employees are 'saboteurs'. This means that in an organization with 1,000 employees, there are some 200 people who would bad-mouth their organization.

Figure 6.2 shows four categories of employee using data from a separate survey:

- *Champions* are the ideal group of employees who both understand and are committed to the firm's goals;

- *Bystanders* clearly understand organizational goals but do not have the emotional drive to support them;

- *Loose cannons* are highly motivated to support business goals but do not understand what they are or how to achieve them;

- *Weak links* are not aware of, or concerned about, business goals.

The 100 best companies to work for in America in 1997, as voted by over 20,000 employees, showed the impact of emotional buy-in on business

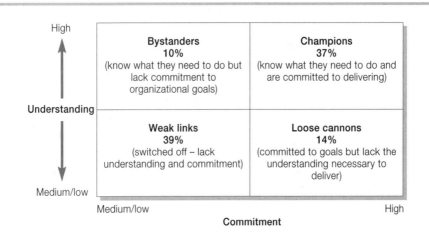

Fig 6.2 ■ Categories of employee by buy-in

performance.[5] Of the 61 companies in the group that had been publicly traded for at least five years, 45 had consistently yielded higher returns to shareholders than industry averages. These 61 companies averaged annual returns of 27.5%, compared with the typical 17.3%. Although the quotations below imply that improved employer brand equity drives business performance, it is probably more complex; the research is mostly based on associations. In other words, the reverse is also likely: namely, better performance inspires more positive employer brand equity. Practitioners will be more concerned with the existence of the virtuous circle than the ideal point at which to enter it.

The link between company performance and employee attitudes

This section is the cornerstone of the chapter. The employee effect on overall company performance is much more marked in some companies than others. Service businesses depend on the relationship between external customers and the staff they meet. At the other extreme, customers dealing with dot.com companies on the Web never encounter anyone. Perhaps they do not have any staff at all. Each board should review the impact of staff attitudes and behaviour on company performance and then decide whether to include the employee segment in their regular review of marketing metrics. If the answer is 'yes' they should ensure that their HR and marketing specialists, and perhaps finance, work together to cross-fertilize techniques.

To contribute to that review, I set out some examples of employee/company performance linkage. There has been some debate as to whether customer and employee satisfaction are linked. Happy employees and customers may not, of course, be doing a lot of business together. They may just be having a great time. Nevertheless the balance of opinion, at least for service businesses, causally links employer brand equity and business performance.[6]

Maryland's Professor Ben Schneider has a framework not dissimilar to MCA's. The three parts are foundation issues (like fairness and trust); how well employees think they are treated; and service climate (emphasis on quality, training and adequacy of resources). Schneider also finds the positive internal/external customer performance link.[7]

In 1997, the Institute of Work Psychology conducted a study of 100 single-site, single-product-operation manufacturing companies with fewer than a thousand employees.[8] According to the study, '12% of the variation between companies in their profitability can be explained by variations in the job satisfaction of their employees. Moreover, 13% … can be explained by the differences between companies in organizational commitment.' Company performance is measured by relative labour productivity (relative to the industry in which the firm belongs) and real profits per employee both before and after the measurement of human resource management practices, culture and attitudes.

Cranfield's Professor Adrian Payne researched the linkages between attraction, satisfaction and retention across the three key stakeholder groups: customers, employees and shareholders. While the majority of the large companies in his and his colleagues' samples collected customer and employee data of these types, their investigation of about 600 UK companies found no examples of British companies *linking* this information to understand what drives what.[9] There are probably few anywhere. The Nortel example of best practice below is taken from their paper.

Nortel Networks

Nortel Networks is a Canadian telecoms company employing 80,000 staff worldwide, with revenues of $18 billion. It benchmarks leading organizations such as Disney and emphasizes quality. It has won US Baldridge and European EFQM awards. Extensive research led the company to its own model, the 'Nortel Business Value Cycle', which explicitly links resources (people, financials, knowledge, partners etc. with customers and ultimately shareholder value. Importantly the feedback loop from shareholder value to resources is labelled 'leadership'.

Establishing such a multifunctional database across a large global business was a major task. On the other hand it has created global organizational learning. A manager in one country, for example, can track the data for a better-performing, but otherwise comparable, unit elsewhere.

Nortel found that leadership accounted for 31% of employee and 18% of customer satisfaction respectively. The required leadership behaviours are clearly identified and monitored. They found that employee satisfaction accounted for 52% of customer satisfaction and are now working on the links between customer metrics and shareholder value.

In recent years, Sears, a major US retailer, has turned its business around by changing its marketing strategy and the nature of its relationships with internal and external customers. They have shown how the employee virtuous circle and high technology to track the data across stores produce both increased customer satisfaction and higher profits.[10] The CEO and a group of top executives developed a business approach for the company to track success from employee attitudes and behaviour through to customer satisfaction and financial performance – an approach they call the 'Employee–Customer–Profit Chain'.

This model represents a new inside-out approach to relationship marketing, as well as a management information system and self-assessment tool. According to Sears executives, 'Our model shows that a 5 [percentage] point improvement in employee attitudes will drive a 1.3 [percentage] point improvement in customer satisfaction, which in turn will drive a 0.5% improvement in revenue growth' (p. 91).

These results are even more compelling when considered against national norms: 'Independent surveys show that national retail customer satisfaction has fallen for several consecutive years, but in the course of the last 12 months, employee satisfaction on the Sears TPI (Total Performance Index) has risen by 4% and customer satisfaction by almost 4% ... an improvement that translates into more than $200 million in additional revenues in the past 12 months ... It is our managers and employees who, at the moment of truth in front of the customer, have achieved this prodigious feat of value creation' (p. 97).

In the hotel and entertainment industries, staff not only provide the ambience and branding, but they are likely to move on quite quickly. Tracking employer brand equity, for example, is quite a problem for Forte.

Forte

Forte Hotels is now part of the Granada group and many changes followed that acquisition. Radan Prayget, Research and Information Controller, reported that the marketing department was split into two sections. One managed the three brands, namely Le Meridien, Posthouse, and Heritage, while the other dealt with the corporate brand, issues common to all brands such as business-to-business and design. The new CEO is from Hertz and is providing a customer-focused model for development, known as 'Commitment to Excellence'.

Metrics are primarily financial (driven by Granada) but there is a strong emphasis on employee motivation using the Sears model. Labour turnover is a key indicator in the hotel business. In addition there is a guest satisfaction survey run by BMRB International and an annual NOP/BDRC awareness survey, along with operational measures of reservation and check-out efficiency. BMRB interviews/telephones 60,000 guests, worldwide, per annum. The balance of metrics now is probably 80% financial and 20% employee and guest satisfaction, though that will move to 70/30.

Granada has had negative experiences from low-cost non-financial metrics and is seeking to adopt a similar measurement system to Forte.

Source: Metrics interview by Shashi Halve with Radan Prayget, 2 March 1999.

More recent UK research, again by MORI on behalf of MCA, showed that dealings with staff ranked third after price and quality in terms of repeat purchase.[11] Unfortunately, 23% of the younger, more affluent consumers are put off by the treatment they receive. Fewer than 50% of all customers felt that staff showed a genuine interest in helping and fewer than 20% claimed that staff showed appreciation for interest or purchase. Fewer than 33% of customers saw employees' commitment to doing their best and only 10% saw pride in goods or services.

In summary, the evidence is that, for a wide cross-section of firms, employer brand equity is likely to be such an important driver of overall business performance that it should be included within the marketing metrics review process. We turn now to the question of what metrics should be used, first in the simple unitary firm and then the variations required to cope with multiple brands and business units.

The unitary brand and business unit situation

These perspectives bear a striking resemblance to the measurement of innovation health in the last chapter. 'Staff awareness of vision/direction' and 'staff commitment to vision/direction' formed the first two metrics under the leadership heading. But the awareness and commitment applied specifically to the corporate *innovation* goals, whereas we are now dealing with the overall business goals. Nevertheless, it is worth looking to see which of the nine innovation metrics in the last chapter could apply to employees.

The nine were:

- Awareness of goals

- Commitment to goals

- Active innovation support

- Resource adequacy

- Appetite for learning

- Freedom to fail

- No. of initiatives in process

- No. of innovations launched

- Percentage of revenue due to launches in last three years.

The last three are specific to innovation but the others, adapted for business goals in general, could apply equally to employer brand equity. A prime example of a company that involves employees in its goals and keeps them posted on progress is the TNT distribution company, which achieved 59% organic revenue growth, and doubled profits, in a mature market that only grew 7%.

TNT

Since 1993, TNT strategy has been based on engaging the whole company in achieving the 'Perfect Transaction Process' to provide everything the customer requires. Every customer is targeted six-weekly with contact and needs analysis.

Every employee is bonused on profit, which encourages all of the 150 profit centres to be entrepreneurial and customer-focused. Employees are surveyed annually by mail with a 65% response rate. Depot awards, league tables and frequent customer care campaigns unify staff in customer focus and values.

All criteria from price competitiveness to staff attitudes are measured six-monthly, against targets, from national to depot levels.

Source: The whole company ... **Designed** *for customers*, The Marketing Council (1999), Cookham, Berks.

An alternative approach is to follow the 'employee as customer' logic and adapt the proposed consumer universal list as follows:

■ *Relative satisfaction.* This presumes the board has employee satisfaction data from peer companies. Year-to-year trends in own employee satisfaction would also be useful.

■ *Commitment.* The determination to achieve the marketing goals as understood.

■ *Relative perceived quality.* Again the calibre of the employer needs to be benchmarked against the calibre, as perceived by their employees, of comparable firms.

■ *Relative price.* In the employee situation, this refers to the compensation package. We know that higher levels of pay do not necessarily cause higher levels of performance but any perceived unfairness will demotivate. And bonuses and incentives especially need to reflect contribution.

■ *Availability.* How easy is it to get to work? Are there opportunities for work sharing/telecommuting?

Relative price is an objective measure of comparable compensation packages whereas satisfaction (above) is attitudinal. In the employee context they should not be merged, but relative satisfaction probably includes relative perceived quality, which could be reduced to diagnostic status for examination when satisfaction rises or falls. Similarly, employee satisfaction and fun place to work probably overlap, though the latter is likely to be a stronger determinant of innovation health.

Combining the first six innovation with the five consumer measures gives ten metrics (commitment appears twice). Active innovation support can probably be generalized as part of overall employee work satisfaction. I am inclined to drop availability from the short list as being more a consideration for potential employees than a metric for those who have found a way to get to work. In some circumstances, a firm may wish to survey employee attitudes against potential employees they would like to engage. Availability (access) would be a useful metric for this purpose. Thus we are left with eight at this stage:

Table 6.2 ■ Provisional short list of employer brand metrics

Awareness of business goals

Commitment to business goals

Perceived resource adequacy

Appetite for learning

Freedom to fail

Relative satisfaction

Relative perceived quality

Relative price (compensation)

For comparison, the approach taken by BP before their merger with Amoco is shown below:

BP

In recent years, BP has researched brand matters with its own staff. In 1997, for example, they found a sophisticated understanding of the BP brand model, audiences and financial objectives. Staff were constructive on how the presentation of the model could be improved and used to manage their external relationships.

The attributes of BP as a brand were tested on four bases: BP today and in the future as an oil company, BP with a new central purpose and the BP they wanted to work for. These four were tested with 28 attributes (plus others) ranging from agile, ambitious and arrogant through to successful, sustainable, technology-led and vibrant. Respondents were asked to circle the five most relevant attributes for each of the four versions of BP.

Finally they were asked some quite direct questions, e.g. whether the company should invest more in the brand.

This was how the results were reported back by e-mail (but the attachments are not shown here):

To: BP Global Brand survey participants

Your participation in the Brand survey is appreciated. The survey results helped shape an understanding of the role Brand plays within BP and provided a very useful basis for continuing discussions.

Some of you will have seen the survey results presented in Group Leadership meetings. The following is a summary of the key results from the survey:

- People within BP demonstrated a good understanding of Brand and agree with the hypothesis that Brand = behaviour.
- There is a widespread awareness of, and commitment to, the importance of Brand.
- There is a thirst for a clearer expression of BP's Brand and a simple communication of it to all employees.
- Emotional content of the Brand is missing.
- Financial objectives drive the culture of the company. We are proud of the fact that we have exceeded challenging targets quarter after quarter. We do not want to lose that part of our identity.
- However, BP is viewed as cold and matter of fact. There is a desire to see a balance with more human/emotional values in the future.
- Attachment 1 illustrates the attributes most associated with BP today.
- Attachment 2 portrays the results when respondents were asked which characteristics they would like to have associated with your BP.
- Attachment 3 illustrates those attributes which are most different in the portrayal of BP today and your BP.
- There is a hunger for action.

The survey results have been used along with the work of the Global Brand Team and discussions with senior managers to form a characterization of BP as embodied in the BP Brand. This characterization is being honed and validated through external research and internal leadership meetings. It is anticipated that this work will culminate in a 1998 Brand Plan resulting from discussions with the Group Executive in New Orleans and the Main Board at the end of this month.

Thank you again for your help and support in this effort.

Source: Duncan Blake, BP Amoco, January 2000.

Even today in the merged BP Amoco, the detailed results of this research are confidential, but the quotation illustrates the imaginative way that BP Amoco uses employee data both as a proxy for consumer research and as a way to establish the directions needed for internal and external marketing.

The multi-brand situation

So far we have considered the unitary situation where the employer, or corporate, brand is the only one sold to customers by the employees. Unitary brand companies have an advantage in aligning the interests of consumers, trade, employees and shareholders. Ideally, the employees are the ambassadors for the brand.

Where a business unit handles many brands, as is the case in Unilever or Mars, each member of staff cannot simultaneously be an ambassador for all the product brands and also the corporate brand. The consumers may not even be aware of, still less care about, the corporate brand and shareholders may care little about some of the product brands. If we accept that what is in the employees' heads is part of brand equity, then measuring employees' mindsets for each of the product brands becomes immensely complicated. And measuring just the top brands risks telling employees that the others do not matter. It is a bit like the naïve application of the shareholder value enthusiasm, which kills all products between the new with golden prospects (stars) and the cash cows. New products cannot become mature if they are not allowed to transit the dark nights between launch and glory.

Alternative solutions to this conundrum of how the employees' share of the intangible marketing assets can be estimated include:

- As far as the *employee* is concerned, loyalty is to the employer, i.e. the corporate brand. We should therefore measure just employer brand equity, as in the section above, and disregard the product brands, be they goods or services.

- Conversely, we could take the view that, from a market perspective, only the product brands matter. The equity of the corporate brand has no significance. For example, when International Distillers and Vintners Ltd was formed as a quoted company in 1962, the directors chose the name precisely because it was undistinguished and unmemorable. They did not want any corporate name that would distract attention from the product brands like J&B Rare, Gilbeys Gin and Smirnoff Vodka.

■ As a mid-position, one could decide that the corporate brand is just another brand and add together what is in the employees' heads about all these brands.

None of these solutions is wholly satisfactory and, as the next section shows, the last solution risks consolidating apples and oranges. The corporate brand is a different kind of fruit.

In practice, the short list of metrics suggested above brings its own solution. Reviewing the eight short-listed employer brand metrics in Table 6.2 shows that none needs to be changed in principle, even though the details may be more complex. The goals, for example, are likely to be more diverse in a multi-brand unit but awareness of, and commitment to, those goals remain paramount. The cultural metrics (appetite for learning, and freedom to fail) do not vary, presumably, by product brand. Similarly the two employment metrics (relative employee satisfaction and relative compensation) are corporate- not product-branded. In effect this eliminates the second of the three options above.

How then do we deal with the product brand issues? Suppose the employees now think that Product A is wonderful but think that B is abysmal, whereas one year ago they were both thought to be equally moderate. If the two brands have really performed equally well, the (internal) marketing of A has been better than B and this, especially in a service business, would impact consumer brand equity in due course. Assessing internal marketing purely in terms of the corporate brand, and ignoring product brands, would entirely miss these key facts.

This forces us to modify the eight metrics for the unitary brand too. Relative compensation and resource adequacy can both be downgraded to being diagnostics of relative employee satisfaction, leaving space for an employee perception of customer value from the leading brand. In the unitary case, that is also the employer/corporate brand. In other words, the metric forces some degree of customer empathy and asks whether the customer really benefits from the brand. We are asking 'Does the employee truly care about what the customer cares about?'

That is quite a complex, albeit important, concept, which I will call 'customer brand empathy'. It includes the relative perceived quality of the firm's brands. In the hypothetical case above, A would score well and B badly. While aggregation would lose important data, a ruthless restriction of the number of metrics a board can review would require us to combine the customer brand empathy scores for, say, the leading brands which make up 80% of shareholder value. This means that a few leading brands will be included and the tail excluded. Diagnostics should be available should more detail be required. As noted above, this risks employees' drawing the conclusion that the minor brands do not matter. Some specific attention would need to be given to that.

Using the BP example above, which was then a single brand, it would have been possible to index how well the employees' responses matched those of consumers to the same brand questions.

The eight metrics then become the seven in Table 6.3:

Table 6.3 ■ Employee multi-brand metrics

Awareness of goals
Commitment to goals
Appetite for learning
Freedom to fail
Relative employee satisfaction
Aggregate customer brand empathy
(Composite index of the extent to which employees see company brands as consumers do)

Can business units be consolidated?

Even if innovation health and employer brand equity are close enough to integrate at the business unit level, all the business units should not be added together. Different parts of the group will perform better and worse in employer brand equity terms and the opportunity for cross-learning will be lost if the metrics are aggregated. This last section reviews this problem of how a large organization can take an overview without losing information. The most important units should be reviewed individually with some summary measures for the remainder.

The group chief executive, or the main board, is likely to want to review innovation health or internal marketing across the whole organization. A large organization may have 100 business units and 3,600 brand market segments. Aggregating the differences will lose the key information about each unit and the totals may be meaningless. There is no easy solution and our research indicates that the top boards of many large companies have simply abdicated: marketing is seen as a matter for the subsidiaries who should monitor their own marketing performance. The top board will reserve its attention for the serious matter of financial performance. As noted at the beginning of this book, most senior marketers regard this, quite simply, as wrong. If a group is too large for the top executives to understand where the money is coming from, the shareholders should break it up.

Whether separate business units can be aggregated depends on how similar they are. For example if, when employees are asked about 'the boss', they always mean the group chief executive, aggregating leadership perceptions is fine. If, however, each employee understands 'the boss' to mean the leader of his or her own business unit, then aggregation makes no sense.

The marketing scientist would determine which business units cluster into similar sub-groups and aggregate those. For example, it might be possible to cluster a group of 100 business units into seven sub-groups, A–G, each with similar units but each sub-group being different to the others. Thus metrics could be reported for sub-groups A–G, e.g. Nordic companies, Southeast Asian companies and so on (whether Nordic countries are that similar to each other is beside the point of this example). Establishing which units are alike is an empirical matter. The rule is simply that similar business units, and brand market segments, can be aggregated, whereas different ones should not be.

The problem does not rest there; the units that are similar in year one may not be in year five.

Nevertheless, global groups need some levels of aggregation if only for the 80% of brand market segments that probably account for only 20% of shareholder value. We are steeped in geographic boundaries and yet it is absurd that the US, which for many categories is about half the world's market, should be treated as a single business unit just like each of the other 200 countries.

Aggregating innovation health and internal marketing metrics is not only possible but desirable. The overlap is considerable: both deal with the same segment (staff in a business unit) and the recommendation is to use the services of a specialist data collector who can benchmark the measures with comparable firms and historical indicators. The goals just need to be broadened to include both innovation and other market goals, and the adequacy of resources for innovation to be added.

As is the case for innovation, most boards should consider an occasional major audit using many more indicators than the few used for regular review. That audit should help determine which employer brand metrics are the most appropriate for that particular business.

A final thought: just as the provision of metrics for the board presents an opportunity to rethink the relationship between marketing and finance functions, so employer brand equity provides a bridge between marketing and human resources (HR). The first shows how marketplace measurement leads to shareholder value and rewards financial capital. The second shows how treating employees as customers rewards human capital, which in turn benefits both customers and shareholders. To do that, HR need marketing skills and marketers need to understand and work with HR. Too often, internal communications are seen as simply passing down information, and too little concern is given to how or if these messages are received and what effects they have. Periodic surveys of staff morale are unrelated to marketing goals, communications or employer brand equity.[12]

For many large companies, finance, HR and marketing operate as separate functions, perhaps even silos, communicating internally but barely with each other. Marketing metrics at board level can *unite the three*.

Executive minutes 6

1 Marketing and HR directors to report on the relative importance of employees as drivers of business performance. To what extent do employees create immediate customer and end user brand equity?

2 HR director to report on specialist firms available to measure employee indicators, costs and experience, on what benchmarking would be available against which peer companies and historical data, and which indicators each firm would recommend.

3 Board to resolve the optimal set of internal employee metrics. Note should be taken of external specialist recommendations (item 2 above).

4 Marketing to report how employees' attitudes and behaviours towards product brands can be included (e.g. aggregate customer brand empathy).

5 HR director to propose how innovation and internal marketing metrics are presented to the board and which business units can be clustered as similar, i.e. how many clusters or subgroups there will be. Finance and marketing directors to comment and, similarly, propose groupings of BMS units.

6 Finance director to include employer brand with other marketing metrics reviews for the board.

References

1 Ambler, Tim and Barrow, Simon (1996) 'The employer brand', *Journal of Brand Management* 4 (3 December), 185–206 defined it as 'the package of functional, economic, and psychological benefits provided by employment, and identified with the employing company'. 'Employer brand equity' is the intangible corporate asset created in the minds of employees by leadership, culture and employment practices.

2 This section is taken, with permission, from Thomson, Kevin and Arganbright, Lorrie (1999) 'The buy-in benchmark: how staff understanding and commitment impact brand and business performance', CIM seminar on Measuring Marketing Performance, May.

3 Arganbright, Lorrie and Thomson, Kevin (1998) 'The buy-in benchmark', the Marketing & Communication Agency Ltd and Market & Opinion Research International: London.

4 Schweiger, David and Denisi, Angelo (1991) 'Communication with employees following a merger: a longitudinal field experiment', *Academy of Management Journal* 34 (1 March), 110–35.

5 Grant, Linda (1998) 'Happy workers, high returns', *Fortune* (12 January), 81.

6 Heskett, J.L.; Sasser W.E., Jr. and Schlesinger, L.A. (1997) *The Service Profit Chain: How Leading Companies Link Profit and Growth to Loyalty, Satisfaction, and Value*, New York: Free Press.

7 Schneider, Ben; White, S.S. and Paul, M.C. (1998) 'Linking service climate and customer perceptions of service quality: test of a causal model', *Journal of Applied Psychology* 83 (2), 150–63.

8 Patterson, Malcolm G.; West, Michael A.; Lawthom, Rebecca and Nickell, Stephen (1997) *People Management, Organisational Culture and Company Performance*, the Institute of Work Psychology, University of Sheffield, and the Centre for Economic Performance, London School of Economics.

9 Payne, Adrian; Holt, Sue and Frow, Pennie (1999). 'Relationship value management: exploring the integration of employee, customer and shareholder value', 7th International Colloquium in Relationship Marketing, Strathclyde University, 7–9 November.

10 Rucci, Anthony T.; Kirn, Steven P. and Quinn, Richard T. (1998) 'The employee-customer-profit chain at Sears', *Harvard Business Review* 76 (January–February), 82–97.

11 MCA/MORI (1999) 'The brand ambassador benchmark' – reviewed by Mitchell, Alan (1999) 'Customer satisfaction is earned by loyal staff', *Marketing Week* (10 June), 38–9.

12 See Thomson, Kevin (1998) *Emotional Capital*, Oxford: Capstone, for examples and substantiation.

7

Supplying the metrics

The previous three chapters assisted the board in selecting the firm's external market, innovation health and employer brand metrics. Gathering the required data, however, is another matter: it is neither straightforward nor easy. This chapter reviews the idealized information supply situation and then some of the real-world difficulties. Getting the data is only a start: marrying it together is the challenge considered in the last section.

As every experienced marketer knows, large company life is complex. When mid-level marketers were asked, in the course of the Metrics research, what they considered to be the single largest impediment to better marketing performance, we received many answers. Money, perhaps surprisingly, was not high on the list. The most frequent response, in large companies, was the difficulty in gaining cross-functional support.

What is true for marketing plans will be even more true for data gathering. It may take months to review and choose the metrics, gather them from diverse sources and run them in. Marketers have neither the manpower nor the muscle to draw the data from other departments and present them consistently. Recent years have seen support staff stripped from marketing, especially from junior levels. Assistant brand managers are rare today. Furthermore, few senior marketers, with an in-post expectation of 18 months, plan to be around that long, nor can a market research firm supply a complete package. Some research firms have many different customers within a single large corporation, each interested only in their particular needs. With marketers not falling over themselves to be measured, and perhaps found wanting, our research reveals a big gap at the top. No one is championing the metrics needed to give an overall picture.

There are stories, apocryphal or not, of consultants being hired by the board to gather the measures from the market but then collecting them from the company's own management silos. This is not as foolish as it may seem: numbers from external consultants carry more credibility than the same metrics from the internal marketers. Consultancy services are now one of the fastest-growing sectors, mainly because middle management use them as conduits to the board and, vice versa, boards use them to get things done that their own management are too busy to do.

Figure 7.1 gives an overview of this chapter, which covers the following key points:

- Auditing your information needs. It is one thing to identify the metrics needed in theory, but quite another to locate and pay for them. The resources allocated to metrics have to be kept in proportion to the marketing they are helping to assess.

- The reality of data supply: the state of market research. Tidy it is not.

- Alignment. Some of the compromise needed when theory hits reality is that metrics will not be perfectly aligned: segments and time periods, in particular, are likely to be more or less inconsistent.

- Packaging metrics for the board. One of the many paradoxes in this metrics game is that the larger the company, the more simple presentation has to become. The problem is not that the board are dumb (they are likely to be smarter than anyone else in the company) – but that they have too little time. Messages have to communicate instantly.

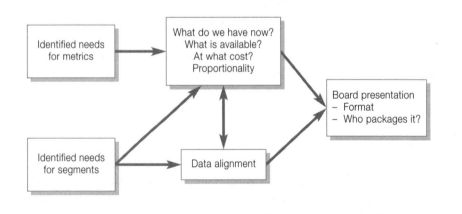

Fig 7.1 ■ Supplying the metrics

- The role of the finance director in overseeing information supply. Metrics come reluctantly and unaligned from many quarters. Marketing directors would be wise not to take a turf stance on this but instead to ask the finance director to take over marketing metrics, including board presentation. This section shows why.

Auditing your information needs

Market research accounts for between 2% and 5% of total marketing expenditure.[1] Attempts have been made to assess scientifically how much each firm *should* spend on information, and in what circumstances, but such studies are unconvincing. The installation, or revision, of board-level marketing metrics should prompt a market research audit to answer these questions:

- Do we already have, somewhere in the company, the data to support the metrics now selected?

- Do we also have the more detailed data that will be needed to answer questions about variances in the metrics (diagnostics)?

- What other information do we regularly receive through tracking studies or surveys?

- What are the lowest costs to obtain what we now need?

- How does the resulting overall cost compare with whatever yardstick the company deems appropriate and with the cost of providing the internal (financial) metrics?

The third question should prompt two subsidiaries:

- What do we now get that can be culled?

- If it cannot be culled, should it be reconsidered for the metrics list, i.e. what is its purpose? What does it add?

Most large companies are buying research that serves no apparent purpose, but they hesitate to cull. Top management questions once asked may be asked again. In-house market researchers accumulate reports like books in a library but, corporate life being what it is, the unceasing stream of newly hired marketers commission new work from ignorance or time pressures or because new work is more credible. Driven by the problem of the week, marketers need information tightly tuned to that particular topic. Academic marketers are no different. Old databases are rarely used for new research.

The data, or information, warehouse has long been regarded as the answer to all this. Marketing information, internal or external, should be stored on the mainframe in some logical order and be available to any manager on a terminal or PC. Those responsible for adding new research or statistics should then ensure that they are accurate and consistent. For example, the 'month' for accounting should be the same as the 'month' for measuring consumer sales. The segment used for measuring awareness should be the same as the segment identified for advertising.

The warehouse could supply top-level information (metrics) with analysis by time, region, stock-keeping unit (individual product pack), customer etc. Software could generate graphs, pie charts and histograms and run regressions. Data mining could, in theory, help target mailings to ever more tightly defined groups, as Tesco is demonstrating with its Clubcard data by sending over 60 segmented mailings to identified groups of customers.

However, this ideal of a single global and comprehensive marketing database has rarely, if ever, been implemented outside the e-commerce, high-tech world of Amazon and Dell. It is especially difficult across national boundaries. Nevertheless it is an ideal worth holding on to as companies move in that direction. The Shell example shows a major trader developing an increasing range of marketing measures worldwide.

Shell

Shell's 'Global Brand Tracker' provides metrics and diagnostics for their brand versus competitors since 1997 across 70 countries. A very wide range of interview questions includes:

- Spontaneous awareness
- Trial
- Purchase
- Loyalty
- Avoidance
- Preference
- Image
- Formula 1 (racing)
- Familiarity
- Favourability.

As trends emerge, the database is proving increasingly useful. Preference and convenience interact, for example, to provide insights into loyalty. The data is used to provide scorecard measures, marketing planning, portfolio decisions (extend/cull) and broad insights at the macro level.

The scorecard shows, for Shell and competitors, the key brand image (intermediate) and behavioural indicators, market and store share, pricing and composite ratios.

Source: Simon Saville, Global Brands Standards Manager, Shell, presentation to the Centre for Marketing workshop at London Business School, 24 November 1999.

The reality of data supply

This section makes the point that the market research industry is complex, untidy and geared to supplying detailed figures for particular problems. They are more interested in the technicalities and efficiencies of their own production process than in providing any board with an overview of its marketing. Ironic as it may seem, the market research industry is not market- or at least consumer-oriented. Few are particularly concerned, according to Robert Heath, Managing Director of Icon, with their *customers'* needs. They are reluctant, for example, to interpret the data they provide. If you agree with this paragraph, skip the rest of this section. If not, read on.

The data warehouse ideal organizes information coherently but it does not address a key difficulty for modern marketers in large companies: data glut. This rather undermines the concept that marketers sit scanning the market and are driven by what they see. In practice they are driven by whatever problem has got to the top of the managerial heap.

So to portray the data warehouse as an information iceberg with metrics being the 10% visible to the board and the submerged 90% being readily available diagnostics, is a nice metaphor but far from reality. Information is problem-driven and if the problems are routinized, so are the research reports. For example, since the 1930s ACNielsen has made a good living out of supplying marketers with, essentially, sales diagnostics. Shortfalls in sales performance could be pinpointed back to the sales person responsible without the need for internal statistics. ACNielsen, then and increasingly now, supplies more market information than this, but its early success was due to the routine need to explain sales variances to top management.

So the problem defines the type of information needed and the marketer goes to the market research firm that supplies that particular type.

Market research is quite a small industry, which supplies a wide range of services: its total published turnover of £0.5 billion is only about 4% of total advertising spend.[2] Accordingly there is a high degree of specialization with relatively low, albeit keen, competition in each niche.

The specialization is both vertical, i.e. according to industry sector, and horizontal, according to the type of research technique employed. Examples of vertical specialization include research agencies – or divisions of agencies – that are entirely devoted to studying the automotive market or the pharmaceutical market.

Specialization can pay off handsomely. It is a little-known fact that the world's second-biggest research agency, after ACNielsen, is IMS Health, which concerns itself mainly with the pharmaceutical industry and monitors global sales of medicinal drugs.

Other agencies concentrate wholly or partly on media research, which has become a highly complex and technical field of study, particularly as far as the measurement of television audiences is concerned. In the United States Nielsen Media Research, now entirely independent of its progenitor, ACNielsen, a giant in its own right, is becoming part of an even bigger group, Dutch publishing house VNU.

In Britain such leading agencies as Taylor Nelson Sofres, which has for many years handled the BARB (Broadcasters' Audience Research Board) TV contract, and Ipsos-RSL, which has done likewise for the National Readership Survey, owe much of their income to their expertise in this area.

Examples of horizontal (technique) specialization include, again, Taylor Nelson Sofres and ACNielsen. The former has huge experience of using consumer panels to measure brand shares of markets; the latter, like its great rival, Information Resources, is best known for the collection and analysis of retail data.

Some agencies, such as Research International, pride themselves on the methods they have developed for assessing the potential size of the market for new products. They have also invested in new thinking and models relating to brand equity (understanding what comprises brand equity and tools for tracking it) and customer loyalty (what builds customer retention and what reduces it). Others, such as Millward Brown and Hall & Partners, are known principally for their continuous tracking of public awareness of brands and advertising.

Several, including MORI and Gallup, have won fame through conducting political opinion polls, though that is usually only a small part of their business. Very many, often quite small, agencies concentrate on so-called focus groups to produce hypotheses about public attitudes to different questions.

Big or small, most agencies have imitated their clients to the extent of offering branded 'products', which more often than not are essentially similar to services available from their competitors. Branding of research services does not, incidentally, save the agencies from having to compete fiercely on price when pitching for new business.

The paradox is that, while market research has been steadily growing as an industry over the past thirty years, and greatly expanding the range of its clients, market researchers have been losing influence as a source of business advice.

The growth is real and impressive. World expenditure on market research is estimated to have totalled $11 billion in 1997, of which 37% was spent in the US itself and 10% in the UK, which has a large research industry relative to the size of its economy. It is noteworthy that the advertising and marketing services group WPP consistently reports that its research subsidiaries are among the fastest-growing parts of its business (18% in the first quarter of 1999 against 5% for advertising).

Diversification of the client base in the industry is likewise impressive. Whereas in the 1960s research clients were mainly manufacturers of packaged goods, they now comprise companies and non-commercial organizations of all types, from charities to tour operators.

As for the decline in influence, one reason is that there are now so many more research agencies, busy with so many more tasks than thirty or forty years ago, that individual research experts no longer wield the clout that some – a George Gallup or an Ernest Dichter in the US, a Mark Abrams or a Harry Henry in the UK – once did. Another reason is that much research is today commissioned on a project-by-project basis, with rival agencies tendering for each project rather than being hired as long-term business partners.

Then again, it is hard to give sound advice if you do not know the full picture, and it is hard to get the full picture if you are unable to talk directly to senior management. Indeed market researchers have long bemoaned their lack of board access and the way they have been pushed down the reporting line. Where large client companies are concerned, research agencies commonly deal with research managers, who themselves are not board members and are considered by their own directors as organizers and suppliers of data rather than as business decision-makers.

The marketing director who attends research debriefs, or focus groups, has become a rarity. Cause and effect are hard to separate. The question is whether declining board-level interest resulted from the researchers' obsession with their own methodology or whether researchers have been pushed back into low-overhead data production by lack of senior managers' attention.

Or is it that researchers, like advertising agents with similar complaints, have been upstaged by the new breed of management consultants, sprung from the loins of accountancy firms, which have always, and for obvious reasons, had the bosses' ears? I suspect, however, that this is more discussed than real and that strategic marketing is a small share of the major consultants' businesses.

There will be no simple general answer and researchers come with all kinds of skills and motivations. Nevertheless the gap that has opened between data supply (production) and board-level requirements is providing the opportunity for specialist firms like the Henley Centre and Icon and consultants like Bain to provide the links, i.e. the metrics.

Only in certain areas, it is suggested, do client companies tend to look to mainstream research agencies for interpretation and advice. One area is advertising effectiveness, where apart from the raw sales data the client often has little to go on but research findings.

Gaining ground but losing influence

Research agencies can take some comfort from a survey carried out in the summer of 1999 among large British companies in which 77% of those companies said they considered that the agencies they used made a significant contribution to their marketing strategy. However, this finding was not quite such good news for the agencies as might be at first supposed.

The same survey, carried out by FDS Market Research International for *Market Research News* (www.mrnews.com) found that, while 73% of respondents expected to make greater use of market research in future, they did not necessarily expect to buy it from research agencies.

Of the sample 28% expected research agencies as such to lose ground against management consultancies and other sorts of consultancy. Only 21% expected the research agencies to gain ground. Among those who expected them to lose ground the reasons most commonly given included the greater effort made by consultancies to understand their clients' business and their ability to offer a wider range of services.

When it came to comments on particular research agencies, the survey threw up some interesting material. For example, 24% of clients of one very large agency thought it showed very good knowledge of their business sector, 24% fairly good knowledge and 24% fairly poor or very poor knowledge.

Asked about the level at which they communicated with the same very large agency, 60% of clients answered senior management and 10% said the marketing director. Another 30% said it depended on the project. In no case was the managing director of the client company involved in dealing with the agency.

In the US, there has been discussion of the market research industry's meeting clients' needs better by packaging data in models for each marketing usage. In other words, a research company would supply one package for overall marketing assessment, another for pricing decisions and so on. This would respond to the problem-driven nature of marketers' research needs and it would syndicate the costs not only of the data but of the expensive and rare technical modelling skills. How far this has really developed in the US is obscure and there is little sign of it in the UK.

Be that as it may, data supply's being driven by many discordant problems and managers is at the root of the difficulty for the board, which requires a single consistent market overview. Market research is commissioned on the basis of each manager's personal knowledge and published specializations. These managers are not just in marketing. Customer satisfaction and complaints may be directly measured by logistics or sales. The customer segments and competitive benchmarks they specify may differ from marketer perceptions.

On the face of it, no such difficulty should exist with internal data, largely financial and under the control of the firm itself. In practice it is not so simple. Internal monthly cut-off dates do not correspond with calendar months or rest of the market. Cost allocations change as well as the level at which the 'bottom' line is taken. The treatment of allowances, discounts and rebates changes from year to year. And the list continues.

Many of these details are not significant and may best be ignored. Where they do intrude, however, boards need to think about the extent to which variances are questioned and who has to separate the technical glitches from the real (market) ones. The final section here takes us back to process: who should package and, where necessary, unravel the metrics?

Alignment

The selection of the audiences, or segments, to be measured can be a more subtle business than selecting the metrics themselves. On the one hand comparability requires consistency from year to year. As noted above, it is the *change*, not the absolute number, that is important. Yet circumstances will change. One solution to this is to collect all possible metrics for all possible segments, including not just customers but also employees, influencers, shareholders etc. This provides diagnostics for middle management who then select the metrics to present to the board. This process, however, risks bias and non-comparability. The Metrics research did not find examples of it in practice and it may be more theoretic than real. Quite apart from straining the market research budget and IT system, managers might not be able to cope with the ensuing information avalanche.

In practice, brand market segment alignment from goals through plans to assessment, and year-to-year continuity, is difficult. Even where all internal and external metrics are available at segment level, the exact boundaries differ from metric to metric and BMS to BMS. Firms can only buy the market research that is available, and internal figures only record what trade sales are made, not the sales made by customers. Retail businesses aside, the differences can be crucial. As markets and marketing develop (or managers change or their minds change), target segments are redefined. One year may prioritize customer retention, widely seen as the most cost-effective form of marketing, whereas another year may target new customers and increased market share.

Full formal segmentation will thus be seen as an expensive luxury for most companies, who are still wrestling with integrating marketing as a whole. The more important aspect of segmentation, which applies to everyone, is alignment. The goals, the target market, the research and the results should all be focused on the same group of people. At the very least, make sure that you are not advertising to one group and measuring another.

Companies should strive to harmonize measurement systems and metrics worldwide. Flexibility of the marketing mix to adapt to local customers is one thing, but localizing measurement is another. The market research industry shows a trend towards reconciling market research standards and measures globally. The reason is simple: a global firm suffers greater overheads, but those should be offset by greater organizational learning opportunities. What works in one market can be tried in another.

But for this learning to operate, comparisons need to be made, i.e. measures need to be comparable. Recognizing that hard-line metrics standardization may inhibit innovation and stifle development, the term 'harmonization' is preferred, which implies some flexibility, as Nestlé and others permit, but not to the point that communication is obscured.

Packaging metrics for the board

In our interviews with large, cutting-edge companies, we expected respondents to agree that boards should create the *climate* for effective marketing, but leave variance chasing to others. However, with rare exceptions, this was not the response we received. Obviously the board of a small company must be hands-on, but the boards of multi-divisional companies were expected by their senior managers (our respondents) to dive into detail too.

Not only should boards seek answers for marketing variances, we were informed, but they should do so promptly. Our suggestion that large companies should apply the learning to next year's plan was also rebuffed. The majority message was 'think small and think for today'. This may well be right, but it raises governance issues concerning the different roles of directors and managers. Some respondents, however, did report greater empowerment with regard to which detail was delegated, and the board used information to determine how well the system worked.

If marketers' perception is that board information will only be followed by demands for detail and double-guessing, then the lack of enthusiasm that we have witnessed for metrics makes sense. Information will only make trouble. Marketers know overall marketing assessment is important but they are reluctant to create rods for their own backs. 'Like turkeys voting for Christmas', someone noted at one seminar. Maybe they should: Christmas is the reason turkeys exist.

Perhaps this section should be retitled 'Packaging the board for metrics', as the emphasis thus far is on the need to use them responsibly. Where a specialist marketing function exists, the role of the board is to encourage it to be more effective by removing road blocks, not to create new ones. And still less to ask about the variances the marketers will already have addressed.

How can that happy state of trust come about?

We are now moving from best current practice to speculation about the future. One of our most encouraging findings was the extent to which internal finance and marketing functions have moved closer. Marketers have learned, and use, financial language and disciplines. Accountants are now keen to understand marketing. They certainly recognize that everything cannot be explained by financial numbers. The Institute of Chartered Accountants of England and Wales (ICAEW), for example, has recently commissioned London Business School to report on brand stewardship: in other words, how companies report on marketing performance and brand equity otherwise than in the formal accounts. Sir Bryan Carsberg, the Secretary of the international accountancy-rule-setting organization, said, 'We do not account for intangibles very well and perhaps cannot do so under traditional accounting.'[3] The widely adopted Balanced Scorecard was devised by two professors of accounting.[4] The ICAEW, when making proposals for reporting on shareholder value, recommended that five of the nine metrics be what we would recognize as non-financial marketing metrics, and the financial metrics largely coincided with ours too.[5]

Table 7.1 ■ Performance indicators recommended in the ICAEW report

Non-financial	Financial
Market share	Revenue growth
Market growth	Economic profit
Customer retention	Return on capital
Customer satisfaction	Market/customer profitability
Price premium	

It is a small step from here to integrating the informational roles of the finance and marketing chiefs. I have written elsewhere about the difficult role of internal market research departments: their crucial independence of mind sits uncomfortably with being part of the team and justifying what that team wants to do.[6] Some firms, e.g. Unilever and Mars, already have marketing information and science reporting that are independent of the marketers. At the same time, every board needs someone to package and present metrics in a coherent fashion.

Where a separate market information function does not exist, there is much to be said for giving the job to the chief financial officer (CFO):

■ It integrates board information.

■ Finance will have to iron out inconsistencies between and within external and internal information to avoid confusing the board.

■ To present the market data, the CFO will have to understand more about the market and marketing.

■ Finance, through market research, will be more engaged in planning, and better marketing plans, with non-financial goals, should result.

■ More objectivity (OK – perceived objectivity).

■ Finance is better placed and trained to distinguish the purely technical variances from the substantive. Discussion between finance and marketing should eliminate the technical and illuminate the substantive before the variances get to the board.

- It will create a better balance between the presentation of non-financial and financial metrics.

- Market research costs will be treated similarly to internal information, i.e. not included in marketing investment, but allocated in the same way as other information costs.

- The CFO is best placed to assess proportionality in allocating resources to information of all kinds.

- There will be a larger market research budget, or at least one that is not cut mid-year. Impartial as of course they are, CFOs also have a natural reluctance to cut their own.

- When the metrics are presented to the board, the CFO is more likely to be believed than marketing or other functional executives looking for budgets to spend. Many boards, and not without foundation, believe that marketers sometimes move the goalposts.

The idea of integrating internal and external information is not new. IT functions were made part of the FD's remit with mixed results. More recently firms have been creating chief knowledge officers (CKOs) whose role is to provide, group-wide, the total knowledge held in any part of that group, be it stored electronically or in the heads of the staff. Not too many chief *financial* officers are lining up for this responsibility. They are secure in the traditional mindset. Well, that may be somewhat unfair: my point is that all functional roles are changing, and integrating internal with market information by the finance director could be a key step. Compared to the ambitions for CKOs, it is also a small one.

Few firms will, in practice, reassign market research and marketing information from the marketing department to finance. But it should at least be discussed. Better to have marketing metrics presented to the board by an enthusiastic finance director than a reluctant marketer.

Whether these functions are merged or not, a single marketing metrics document needs to reach the board in a timely fashion and with a complete explanation of how the metrics are arrived at as well as the metrics themselves.

Early on, a target for a manageable set of metrics was set, arbitrarily but consistently with respondents' views, at 20 or fewer. The generalized set (Chapter 3) suggested three profit and loss account plus five brand equity. If you add four to tailor the metrics to the firm's unique strategy and nine for innovation and employer brand equity, this gives a total of 21.

This is tight, but a single page can accommodate up to 30 if necessary. Compromise will be needed to reconcile a complete overview with focus.

In a unitary company (one brand in one market), the metrics should occupy a single page and adopt the traffic light system (red, green and amber for worsening, improving and static metrics) for short-term changes. Exceptional longer-term trends can be shown as charts on backup pages. Alternatively, arrows can be added to the traffic lights to indicate the direction of longer-term changes or double derivatives (rate of change of the trend).

Consideration will need to be given to the number of benchmarks for comparison. The best two are plan and the key competitors, but prior year and the total market are alternatives.

A large multi-brand, multinational company will have to be selective about the brands and brand market segments it wishes to review at board level. The balance between consolidation and retaining the precision of brand market segment analysis is an empirical matter, about which the board must make hard choices.

Executive minutes 7

1 Board to appoint CFO, senior executive or external consultant to recommend process for integrating external and internal information into the board's routine marketing metrics report. This should include the timetable for the production of the first marketing metrics report, taking data availability into account, and frequency thereafter.

2 Unless there is a senior information specialist or CKO, the CFO should be put in charge of metrics processing and board presentation.

3 Marketers and finance team to audit market research in the light of the new metrics specification and report on additional costs and savings (as a result of culling redundant research).

4 IT executive to report on the marketing data warehouse concept, how closely it matches the ideal for the company and what progress has been made towards it. If the warehouse concept is not appropriate, he or she should report on how diagnostics will be produced and how the whole system will retain consistency and integrity.

5 Metrics team and other research users to review expectations from suppliers. Are they just buying data or is the supplier communicating intelligence and implications? Should certain suppliers occasionally report on key metrics directly to the board?

References

1 The Marketing Forum 1998, Research Report (16) reports 5% from those on board but they tend to be the larger companies with bigger marketing budgets; 1997 figures from the *NTC Market Pocketbook* show 4% of total advertising expenditure or, by inference, 2% of all marketing expenditure.

2 1997 figures from the *NTC Market Pocketbook*.

3 (1998) 'Future directions of financial reporting', *Performance Measurement in the Digital Age*, London: the Institute of Chartered Accountants of England and Wales, 36–40, 37.

4 Kaplan, Robert S. and Norton, David P. (1992) 'The Balanced Scorecard: measures that drive performance', *Harvard Business Review* (January–February), 71–9.

5 (2000) *Inside Out: Reporting on Shareholder Value*, London: the Insitute of Chartered Accountants of England and Wales (January).

6 Ambler, Tim (1997) *Marketing from Advertising to Zen*, London: Financial Times Pitman, Chapter 26, 280–90.

8

The fuzzy future

This concluding chapter provides the cold water after the sauna of statistics, or metrics, that has gone before. A company cannot be managed by metrics alone. Furthermore, metrics can actually damage performance if not used constructively. The British National Health Service has provided a perfect example of this. When waiting list lengths became a key performance indicator, targets were met by preventing patients from joining the lists. The lists were reduced, but the waiting *times* were increased.

So what is the answer? Part of it, at least, is to be fuzzy about it. Being too clinical kills off the enzymes we need for growth. Figure 8.1 gives an overview.

The first section of this chapter, on the misuse of performance measurement, makes two points: one should not mistake the signals for the business itself. Metrics should probably not, surprisingly, be used for management incentive schemes.

The second section deals with complexity. Piling new metrics on top of old simply confuses, as large companies have too many numbers to review already.

Third, the chapter considers how exact the system should be. Should goals and measures be perfectly aligned? Should they be precise, unambiguous and unchanging? The answer to all these is 'no'. Perfect alignment belongs to the funeral parlour. Dynamic searching for growth, experimentation and innovation all require some degree of misalignment. Too little and too much alignment are equally bad. Companies somewhere in the middle have a difficulty. Should they increase or decrease alignment? And how fast should they change? Without some (but not perfect!) consensus on these issues, experimentation will be needed and that, in turn, requires

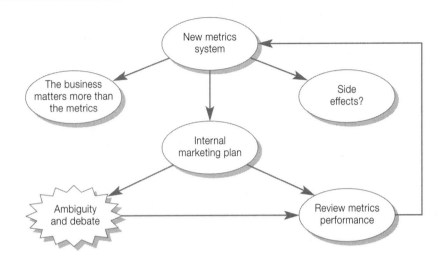

Fig 8.1 ■ The fuzzy future

metrics. The metrics system should support evolution and be constantly changing as part of it. Ambiguity is not some unfortunate lack of precision but an essential ingredient of growth. The future is fuzzy.

The way the marketing metrics system is used is more important than the choice of individual metrics and than the process that delivers them to the board. These tools may be honed to perfection and yet the whole thing will go horribly wrong if the board treats metrics as mechanical levers to drive performance. They are merely crude indicators of the vital signs of a living business.

As usual, the chapter concludes with some key action points.

Misusing measurement

There are many examples of metrics misuse. Lin Fitzgerald of Warwick Business School uses a classic tale of the newly privatized water industry. During successive droughts and water shortages, the public were outraged by leakages left unrepaired. The regulator introduced water leakage reduction as an incentive target. Targets were met but the rate of repairs was little changed. How come? The companies reduced water pressure to place less strain on the pipes. Fire service hoses drooped just as the drought increased the number of fires. In July 1999, the UK train infrastructure monopoly Railtrack announced that top management bonuses would be moved from train punctuality to shareholder returns: but train user groups predicted worse performance from the customer's perspective. My favourite is the Chartered Accountants of England and Wales' performance metrics for board directors.[1] Apparently, directors' attendance records provide the sole measure of directors' performance. Woody Allen is right: 90% of success is just showing up.

We all know the dangers of measuring what is easy to measure. A fuzzy sense of what matters is far more important than precise calculation of the irrelevant. Chapter 3 compared universal measures with developing an original set specifically to fit the firm's goals. Both approaches can be combined but there is danger in making the decision with too little debate. Installing a set of alien measures and moving promptly along to the next burning issue is not efficient management but merely creating a new burning issue for tomorrow.

Any board should know, worry about and constantly revise its model of business success and where the cash comes from. In other words, *why* do customers want to hand over their money? How can that motivation be improved? How can others be persuaded to do likewise? And how can more go to employees (including the board itself) and shareholders? In that cash flow, what are the key signs of vitality and growth? Never mind, for the moment, whether they can be measured or not. If you walked into your own company, knowing nothing, how would you tell which things are going well and which badly? The marketing metrics system is merely a way to maintain those eyes of innocence; it provides signals, not solutions.

The point is that any set of signals gives a partial, lopsided view of the business as a whole. No business should be run solely by numbers. When metrics are given too much importance, they obscure the sense of the business itself.

A popular quick fix is to use the metrics as the base for management incentives. For example, the top five metrics can be weighted to give a single index for bonusing purposes. A more sophisticated version widely used with Kaplan and Norton's Balanced Scorecard is to create such an index but insist that a minimum improvement must be made on *every* one of the top five before any bonus is paid. This at least has the advantage of stopping managers ramping up the easy ones and letting the others go.

Having been there and done that, it seems that using marketing metrics for bonusing is simply a bad idea. Quite apart from the need for ambiguity to which we will revert, the use of metrics for bonuses has five major flaws:

■ They become more important to those managers than the business itself. At the very least they distort it, as noted above. The Balanced Scorecard has spawned many bonus schemes, notably in the US, but not with any apparent success or business improvement.[2] New schemes soon follow.

■ Metrics are only as useful as their credibility. Once suspicion arises that managers may be manipulating them for bonus purposes, their value dries up.

■ Management incentives, at least in the West, are intended to reward individual performance whereas marketing metrics reflect the company's performance as a whole. Metrics have more merit for the board itself and any company-wide scheme.

■ For bonuses, metrics have to be boiled down to a single index. The restrictions, e.g. minimal performance on each metric, serve as negatives rather than motivation. No matter how cleverly it is done, this model oversimplifies business reality. It may be better than using the single index of shareholder value growth but that does not make it good. When bonuses pay out against numbers, whether rigged or not, that do not reflect reality, this unfairness debilitates enthusiasm and motivation.

■ Finally, the use of metrics for control can be demotivating. Reluctance to provide control data to the board is both real and understandable. It provokes criticism and demands for explanation of variances and for more data. This is especially true for innovation, where we were told that KPIs would damage creativity. Using measures for our own professional assessment differs from providing others with sticks to beat us with.

Yet, to my surprise, most of our respondents told us that boards really should behave primarily in control mode. My view remains that self-control beats top-down control. Yes, we know it is necessary, but it can also be destructive to fine marketing. Boards can exercise self-control at two levels: using metrics for their own information and to motivate management to do likewise. Boards of large companies should restrain themselves from excessive variance chasing but provide a culture in which middle management will take care of control.

Shedding the old

Some years ago, a spirits company was remunerating the sales force on the basis of volume sales. With diverse profits per case, values per case and discounting out of control, the quick fix was to remunerate the sales force on gross profit. Sales information was shifted from volume only to show values and margins. The sales team grumbled about losing sales information printout, not because it was better but because they were used to it.

A few years later, the process was reversed. The incoming sales director decided, now that discounts were under control, that this delegation was too sophisticated and sales value was all they needed. Same refusal to give up the old tool.

At a board meeting, the export management were eulogizing about the value of the new information the board had so wisely authorized. There were the figures stacked right beside them. Unfortunately, the paper pile had that virginal, unruffled look of printout untouched by hand.

The moral of these stories, of course, is a marketing one. Metrics are merely the apex of the marketing information system that needs to be understood from the points of view of the various users. Metrics have little value in themselves; their effect depends on how they are used and that, in turn, will be strongly influenced by how other performance measures are used by the board and whether the board is changing. We were told that one of the most frequent reasons for a radical revision of metrics was a change of management: the new team uses new measures in new ways to symbolize and create the makeover they require.

Under these circumstances, shedding the old is almost a condition of continued employment. Where the development is more evolutionary, however, the process of eliminating old measures is more subtle. The installation team, which preferably includes users, needs to show how the new metrics can be used to better effect. A better measure needs to work better just as a better spade needs to help the gardener. Taking the old away arbitrarily is not the answer: it is more important to engage in an active marketing programme that includes board involvement.

The need for misalignment

Innovative companies, such as 3M, recognize the need for experimentation, which implies freedom for managers to explore areas beyond existing strategy. Indeed, by the time a corporate activity is officially enshrined in strategy, it is already middle-aged. Recognition that businesses are now in an era of constant change is hardly new. Yet we seek to install new systems, and align policies and people, as if the firm will never change again. When thinking of changing the metrics system, we have two choices. In one, metrics are perfectly aligned with strategy, and they identify the levers managers should operate to optimize results. The other is fuzzy: metrics are used for broad positioning rather than precision and for illumination rather than control. Table 8.1 compares the present situation, where marketing performance is rarely quantified in the full formal sense, with these two alternative future choices.

Future 1 is precise with perfect alignment and may seem the goal for the quantified approach. Future 2 has the basic measures in place but it is fuzzy.

Table 8.1 ■ Two future metrics scenarios

	Today	Future 1	Future 2
Goals	Mostly implicit	Clear and complete	Fuzzy and incomplete
Key performance measures	P&L account	Balanced Scorecard with precisely identified trade-offs	Financial and market measures both seen as important but trade-offs unclear
Market metrics tied to executive bonuses	No, financial and tasks if any	Yes, as above	No, but influenced by metrics
Goals, performance and metrics	Alignment uncertain	Exactly aligned	Knowingly misaligned
Use of metrics by board	Personal choice	Means to direct and control	Don't know what junior management have to do but wish to provide the tools
Organizational mindset	Habituation	Cognitive/logical/rational	Affective/social/ feelings

Sharing drafts of this table has provoked opposing reactions. Some see Future 2 as common sense and reject the rigidity of Future 1 whereas others do the reverse. In the same company, some executives are more and some less tolerant of fuzziness. These differences are important: the disagreement is part of fuzziness itself. But the continual tussle between alignment, or uniformity, and diversity needs to be open rather than political. It needs to be managed for performance enhancement.

While companies need both points of view, the balance may depend on the corporate life cycle. The young thrusters of a vital new business may be intolerant of the very controls they need. Conversely, the one foot in the grave mature businesses may resist ambiguity. *Rigor*, as they say, is next to *mortis*.

In most companies today, the extent of goals and measures alignment is unknown. Michel Lebas, of the HEC School of Management in France, reports that managers from the same company rate their organization's characteristics across a number of dimensions with little consistency.[3] They are surprised by this but the resulting debate, while reducing the gaps, rarely brings total alignment. What the debate does, and this is important, is to stimulate fresh energy and commitment.

Alignment is another of those upside-down U shapes where too little and too much are both sub-optimal. Some degree of misalignment is essential for experimentation and growth but the company as a whole will only benefit if this, and the experiments, are widely understood. This is why the debate is so important and why the imposition of any set of metrics, however well chosen, is a mistake.

The case for fuzziness is itself fuzzy and should not be wholly accepted or rejected. While fuzziness is superior to the old command and control model now widely derided, your company's need will depend on the current balance between the control and fuzzy cultures and its own life stage.

Executive minutes 8

1 Before installing a new metrics system, the board should consider possible misuse and side-effects.

2 The installation should itself be subject to a marketing plan to ensure that new metrics will be adopted over previous metrics as a matter of board and manager preference, not fiat. Marketers to propose how the new system can be sold in and the old discarded.

3 Although the new system will require at least enough consistency for comparative information and trends to become visible, the new system should allow for continuing evolutionary development. Board to review.

4 Chief executive to establish the internal debate needed to implement the three criteria for assessing the firm's marketing performance measurement system: own and competitive benchmarks and brand equity measurement. Goals and metrics to be aligned, fuzzily, in consequence.

5 Board to ensure that metrics remain subservient to corporate ideology and identifying the firm's vital signs; and that self-controls are preferred to top-down. Board to monitor culture to ensure metrics make the most positive contribution to performance.

References

1   (1999) 'Boardroom governance: practical insights', London: the Institute of Chartered Accountants of England and Wales, 2.

2   Discussion during the Theory of Measurement symposium, Cambridge, UK, 16 July 1999. None of the assembled experts could recall a Balanced Scorecard type of incentive scheme's surviving very long.

3   Lebas, Michel (1999) 'Building the foundations of performance management: from "OR" to "AND", a diagnostic tool', paper presented to the Theory of Measurement symposium, Cambridge, UK, 16 July.

Assessing advertising and promotional campaigns

The book has considered the assessment of marketing expenditure as a whole, but marketers are more often taxed with justifying individual communications (advertising, PR and direct) and promotions campaigns.

This best practice concerns only campaigns supplied externally by advertising or promotional agencies, not price or other activities devised internally. These campaigns may involve all kinds of communications and incentive devices, including price and direct marketing across all business sectors, not just consumer goods. Promotions mostly aim for an immediate effect on trial and/or sales, but communications campaigns have diverse objectives.

This appendix covers:

- The separation of communication and promotion campaigns from the rest of marketing.

- Why assessment matters but does not usually happen.

- Key steps in campaign assessment covering both effectiveness (did it reach the goals?) and efficiency (profitability). Technically, efficiency should be expressed as a ratio of output to input resources, e.g. ROI, but any form of profitability calculation can be treated as efficiency.[1]

- The advantages, dos and don'ts of payment by results.

- A checklist to assess your current system.

- Allocation of costs. Attention is usually given to the results part of the equation but assessors should ensure that only the relevant costs are charged to campaigns and, come to that, to marketing in general. For various historical reasons certain costs, e.g. discounts, have been allocated to marketing even though they do not belong there.

Separation of the marketing mix

Surprising as it may seem, very few advertising and promotional campaigns are assessed to professional standards. As a quick study of any of the ten volumes of IPA Advertising Effectiveness Awards[2] will reveal, recording the objectives and comparing the results is not as easy as it may seem.

The first issue to resolve is whether the campaign can realistically be separated from the rest of the marketing mix. If the budget is more than 90% of the total marketing budget, and if the product and pricing are virtually unchanged, then the campaign and the whole marketing performance are probably too similar to separate.

At the other extreme, if the campaign is a very small part of the whole it may not be worth separating, even if one could.

If the campaign can be separated, it still needs to be evaluated in the context of the rest of the programme. A technique I favour, though it is not much practised, is to expose the marketing plan while still in draft form to the major communications and promotional agencies, and have them compete for resources by setting themselves targets they would achieve if allocated the sums they seek. The attraction of this internal market is that the agencies are fully in the picture for the plan as a whole. They should be encouraged to improve the plan whether it is in their special area or not.

Why assessment matters

- Client and agency have a marketing partnership seeking to achieve the same marketplace goals; only then will they gain their separate benefits;

- Quantifying objectives helps to clarify what client and agency are seeking;

- Clients are increasingly pressed on accountability;

- Doing better in future depends on knowing which campaigns worked best, and why;

- Sharing improves measurement methodology and data;

- Better information gives better overall budgeting and better allocation of mix;

- Successors can learn from their predecessors.

Why assessment does not usually happen

- Many promotions are seen as low-budget items of low interest to top management;

- Lack of relevant research data;

- Isolating results is difficult and time-consuming.

- There are too many different, even conflicting, objectives for each campaign;

- The drive is to get the next job done, and move the game on;

- Junior marketers move on too quickly to make evaluation worthwhile for them;

- Competitive orientation (fill the advertising or promotional slot, never mind how much it improves profits or brand equity);

- Data deluge: large companies have more information than they can use;

- Lack of clarity about agency and client roles and relationship.

The crucial stages for assessment

- Does the agency know what it is supposed to be achieving?

  - Too many creative presentations are rejected due to inadequate briefing.

  - Agency should be briefed on the wider marketing context and overall competitive situation.

  - Is the agency aware of no-nos (things the campaign must not do)?

  - Is there a brand positioning statement?

  - The campaign requirement: the agency should thoroughly understand what the campaign should achieve, as distinct from how to do it (which is the agency's job).

  - How will it recognize 'success'? A very small number of goals, ideally just one, should be quantified. If there are more than one, an importance ranking will help the overall assessment. If prior targets are not the benchmarks, what are? Astonishingly, standard-format agency creative briefs give no space to this most crucial item.

- Were the benchmarks validated against prior campaigns or competitive performance to ensure they were realistic but challenging enough? Effectiveness is not a matter of reaching any old benchmarks. They have to be relevant and difficult but reachable.

■ Most campaign assessment fails because the goalposts were moved, but no one kept a record of this. Jointly revisit and record the goals just before the campaign runs.

■ Was the campaign effective? Comparing results with goals using three kinds of data separation:

- Distinguishing the baseline (what would otherwise have happened) from the campaign uplift.

- Isolating the campaign from the rest of the marketing mix.

- Separating the target segment from the rest of the business.[3]

■ Was the campaign efficient?

- If profit is a key objective, it should have been one of the goals.

- What was the financial return (incremental profit) as a percentage of the campaign cost (ROI)?

- What was the impact on the marketing asset (brand equity)? Note: as discussed in Chapter 1, it is simply wrong to look at profit effects without considering whether brand equity shifted.

- How does this efficiency (ROI) performance compare with other (similar) campaigns, after adjusting for any brand equity changes?

In practice companies rarely have the data and the time to do all this analysis. Unless it is a pilot, one would not invest more than about 10% of the campaign budget in its assessment. Client and agency should agree ahead of time what separations will be made and whether it will be done by collecting hard data or by mutual best guessing. With experience, combining the agency and client estimates is a valuable way of establishing a shared view of the objectives and the results, when hard data is limited.

Where efficiency is not part of the agency brief (profitability is often confidential), that part of the evaluation is likely to be internal, for the client only.

Why payment by results (PBR) is becoming an important discipline for both clients and agencies

■ It is the only effective guarantee that results will be assessed against expectations;

■ It focuses agency efforts on what matters, e.g. creative awards are nice but not primary;

■ It ensures goals are few and precise;

■ Goals need to be shared as part of creative briefing;

■ It maximizes learning and promotes open relationship;

■ The agency should challenge feasibility of goals before implementation;

■ It increases good use of baseline, targeting and isolation analysis;

■ It reflects future intentions (33% of SPCA members saw PBR as the way forward, and it is an increasing part of advertising agency rewards[4]).

Dos and don'ts for payment by results

■ Don't allow it to be simply a way for the client to cut costs, or just a gracious tip to a worthy agency;

■ Agreement to PBR should be deep, not cosmetic;

■ Make sure it is part of a long-term relationship (or the learning will be wasted);

■ Make sure it is part of annual agency/client mutual assessment (see ISBA/SPCA/CIPS model contract);

■ Make PBR a small component until both sides are happy with the way results are evaluated. Then ratchet the PBR component up to an expectation of about 30% of the total agency remuneration so that payments range from 70% to 150% of fee expectation with 100% for on-target performance. There is no reason, despite agency preference, for total expected remuneration to be higher because of PBR.

A checklist to assess your current system

The primary items are at the top of this list, followed by technical factors. After reviewing the stages and technical separations, decide how important each is for your type of business. For example, the separation of the target for the promotion may not be important for those selling direct. If that is the case for this promotion, weigh J as zero. Scores should both be assigned as the percent for each item (100 being perfect). weights should add up to 100%, so that the last column (score x weight) could total to a maximum perfect score of 100%.

Table A1 ■ Assessing your campaign evaluation system (effectiveness)

Stage		Score %	Weight	Total %
A	The briefing process (context and campaign)			
B	Setting baselines and incremental uplifts (goals)			
C	Were the goal revisions noted pre-promotion?			
D	How well was effectiveness quantified?			
E	How well was efficiency quantified?			
F	How full and frank was the mutual de-briefing?			
G	To what extent was Payment By Results used?			
Technical separations:				
H	Baseline (what would have happened without the promotion)			
I	Isolating the promotion from the rest of the mix			
J	Separating the target from the total market			
Total		–	100%	

Establishing an accurate baseline, and therefore the incremental promotional effects, requires a review of changes in the following factors both to set goals and in the event relevant to those expected when goals were set:

■ Environment/market size;

■ Seasonality;

■ Expected competitive (re)actions;

■ Distribution – channels, no. outlets (comparable stores);

■ Pricing;

■ Inventories (pipeline effects).

Similarly, adjustments should be considered for the marketing mix and target market (if one was distinguished from the total business). After multiplying by the weights and then adding up the results to get an overall total, the final figure is the score out of 100. Whether 70%, for example, is good depends on your expectations and how good the competitions are. Firms may wish to use this methodology as a benchmarking tool.

What is 'marketing' expenditure?

What is *charged* to the marketing, or brand, budget varies widely. Most firms *exclude* the departmental, product and packaging costs, but *include* market research expenditure. Promotions are the most difficult area. Price promotions are really discounts and should be charged to sales or discounts and allowances, or be shown as reducing net sales turnover. In practice, a dominant sales management will pressure the marketing team to pick up the tab for any sales costs, including trade (price) promotions where they can.

That said, the brand-building and quick-buck expenditures can be hard to separate. Promotions are often a mix of increased volume, lower price and value-adding components. Or, in the case of advertisers such as furniture and carpet stores DFS and Allied Carpet respectively, the 'sale' advertising should be part of marketing because being low-cost is a key part of their brand equity.

And that is the simple test of what should, and should not, be charged to the marketing (brand) budget: *whether the activity is intended to add to brand equity*. My view is that only those costs that (should) increase the marketing asset should be charged to the brand, i.e. marketing. Analysts and investors are increasingly demanding marketing expenditure in PLC Annual Reports but until that becomes common practice, little consensus will exist. To make the distinction, the first column in Table 3.1 (Chapter 3) shows expenditure as 'marketing investment'.

By the same logic, market research should no more be charged to the brand than should central accounting costs. The cost of information should be separated from brand building, not least because the balance between information and action costs should be kept under review. All information and no action is as foolish as all action without information.

Conclusions

This appendix argues strongly for using an internal marketplace for communications and promotion agencies and for rewarding them with payment by results. It is sensible for agencies to recover their costs but their profits should rely on performance. Through this method, the client gets an improved plan and also outsources most of the campaign assessment problem.

Of course, it is not quite that easy. The client will have to make the tough decisions and provide most of the data. Nevertheless, at a time when marketing departments have been cut while also being pressed to be more accountable, payment by results is the surest way to ensure that the results are assessed.

References

1 This section is based on separate research funded by the Sales Promotion Consultants Association during 1999 and 2000, and on a review of the IPA Advertising Effectiveness Awards for 1998. The promotional research is reported in the Sales Promotion Consultants Association White Paper on promotional assessment, which may be downloaded from http://www.spca.co.uk.

2 The Award winners have been published every two years since 1981 by NTC, Henley on Thames.

3 The creative target (e.g. 25–30-year-old housewife in Manchester with two kids and a Mondeo) should not be confused with the measurement target segment discussed here, i.e. the one used in goal setting.

4 Lace, Jonathan (2000) 'Payment-by-results: is there a pot of gold at the end of the rainbow?', *International Journal of Advertising*, forthcoming.

Appendix

B

Individual metrics

This appendix reports the results of the survey for the top metrics and also those metrics that were discarded due to lack of popular support. Many of these are worth serious consideration, e.g. pipeline and weight ratio.

These metrics assume that trends will be shown in addition to actual measures. Indeed the trends (derivatives) and rates of change of those trends (second-order derivatives) are more important than the snapshot metrics.

Composite measures, e.g. brand strength, and diagnostics, e.g. sales by area or channel (trade customer segment) or (consumer) segment, are also excluded. A number of metrics, e.g. perceived quality, could be treated in their own right (consumer intermediate) or as comparative indicators against the main competitor, the market leader, or the market as a whole. To reduce repetition, the list below mostly allocates a metric either to a stand-alone or to a competitive category.

Table B1 ▦ Top marketing metrics

Metric	% of firms using measure	% that reach their top board	% giving top rating for assessing marketing performance
Profit/profitability	91.5	73.0	80.5
Sales, value and/or volume	91.0	65.0	71.0
Gross margin	81.0	58.0	20.0
Awareness	78.0	28.0	28.0
Market share (volume or value)	78.0	33.5	36.5
Number of new products	73.0	24.0	25.3
Relative price (share of market value/volume)	70.0	34.5	37.5
Number of complaints (level of dissatisfaction)	69.0	30.0	45.0
Consumer satisfaction	68.0	36.0	46.5
Distribution/availability	66.0	11.5	18.0
Total number of customers	65.5	37.4	40.0
Perceived quality/esteem	64.0	32.0	35.5
Loyalty/retention	64.0	50.7	67.0
Marketing spend	64.5	71.3	62.8
Relative perceived quality	62.5	52.8	61.6
Number of new customers	57.0	48.2	57.0
Brand/product knowledge	55.0	41.8	44.5
Image/personality/identity	54.5	43.0	56.0
Shareholder value	52.5	83.8	79.0
Perceived differentiation	50.0	46.0	49.0
Revenue of new products	49.0	55.1	61.2
Relative consumer satisfaction	48.5	55.7	60.8
Relevance to consumer	48.0	42.7	52.1
Penetration	47.5	40.0	46.3
Commitment/purchase intent	47.5	35.8	43.1
Number of leads generated/enquiries	46.5	33.0	44.0
Conversions (leads to sales)	46.5	42.0	54.0
Margin of new products	46.0	55.4	66.3
Price sensitivity/elasticity	45.0	43.3	51.0
Customer satisfaction (trade)	45.0	48.9	57.8
Loyalty (share of category)	43.0	47.7	61.6
Other attitudes, e.g. liking	42.5	38.8	33.0
Purchasing on promotion	39.5	30.4	48.0
Number of products per customer	36.0	29.0	41.7
Share of voice	30.5	34.4	50.8
Per cent discount	30.0	66.7	63.3
Salience (prominence)	28.5	35.0	36.8

Marketing metrics that were considered but did not make the final survey

1	***Market data***	
1.1	Market size/value	

2	***Consumer/end user thoughts and feelings (intermediate)***	
2.1	Ad awareness	Recall and/or recognition of current campaign (not brand awareness)
2.2	Perceived value	Value for money

3	***Consumer/end user behaviour***	
3.1	No. of purchases p.a.	No. of purchases made/no. consumers
3.2	Warranty expenses	Cost of quality rectification
3.3	Target market fit	Actual and target consumer profile match (demo/psychographics)
3.4	Weight ratio	Indicates whether the brand has, on average, heavy or light users. Calculated by: SOM/{penetration × share of category requirements}; WR<1 implies light users

4	***Trade customer/retailer***	
4.1	Cost per contact	Cost of sales call
4.2	Share of shelf	Retailer space as % total
4.3	Features in store	No. of times p.a.
4.4	Pipeline stockholding (days)	Stock in distribution channel
4.5	Out of stock	% of stores with no stock. May be weighted as above
4.6	% sales on deal	% of sales from promotional periods
4.7	Service levels	e.g. on-time delivery

5	***Relative to competitor***	
5.1	Market rank	Competitive position (leader = 1)
5.2	Relative share	% SOM/SOM (Share of Market) of brand leader
5.3	Relative actual quality	Objective functional comparison

6 Innovation

6.1 Satisfaction from new products

7 Financial

7.1 New customer gross margins	Ditto but for recent customers
7.2 New customer acquisition cost	
7.3 Stock cover	Inventory expressed as day's sales
7.4 A/AMP %	Advertising as a proportion of the marketing expenditure

Table B2 ■ Key metrics where responses varied by respondent role

Metric	% of firms using measure	% finance responses	% marketer responses
Awareness	76.5	70.9	90.1
Market share (volume or value)	76.5	72.1	88.9
Number of new products	71.3	76.0	63.0
Relative price (SOM value/volume)	69.6	65.8	75.3
Consumer satisfaction	72.2	63.3	76.5
Distribution/availability	61.7	49.3	79.0
Perceived quality/esteem	65.7	60.0	72.8
Loyalty/retention	67.0	54.4	76.5
Marketing spend	68.7	57.0	84.0
Number of new customers	60.0	53.2	66.7
Brand/product knowledge	57.0	39.2	76.5
Image/personality/identity	55.2	43.0	74.1
Perceived differentiation	53.5	41.8	64.2
Revenue of new products	51.7	43.0	65.4
Relative consumer satisfaction	50.9	43.0	58.0
Relevance to consumer	50	34.2	66.7
Penetration	49.1	45.6	65.4
Commitment/purchase intent	50.9	38.0	65.4
Number of leads generated/enquiries	49.1	43.0	54.3
Conversions (leads to sales)	49.1	38.0	55.6
Margin of new products	48.7	41.8	59.3
Price sensitivity/elasticity	47.8	44.3	55.6
Other attitudes, e.g. liking	44.8	29.1	63.0
Purchasing on promotion	40.4	24.0	63.0
Number of products per customer	36	25.3	53.1
Share of voice	32.6	16.5	54.3
Per cent discount	34.3	21.5	45.7
Salience (Prominence)	32.6	19.0	46.9

Note: Any seeming discrepancies between role splits and overall frequency values is due to the 'Other' role category.

Supplement to innovation health metrics (Chapter 5)

This supplement first notes the better-faster-cheaper process measures proposed by Voss et al. Then some objections to innovation health metrics are noted and I give reasons for their rejection. This left the long list of 38 innovation health metrics which was reduced by further discussions with practitioners to yield the short list in Chapter 5.

The Voss process measures

'Better' measures:

- **Formality.** All innovations have to follow the same broad process and everyone knows what it is.

- **Organization** should be flat and informal.

- **Incentives,** not necessarily financial, should be seen to reward success. For example innovators are promoted.

- **Delegation.** Once the targets are agreed, senior management should get out of the kitchen.

- **Diversity.** Multifunctional teams should have a wide mix of skills, personalities and backgrounds. The mixed evidence on this shows diversity to slow the process at least initially. Accordingly diversity should be set by the nature of the required innovation and not by political correctness.

- **Supplier and customer involvement.** Retailers often lean heavily on their suppliers for innovation. Conversely, in business-to-business marketing, innovation is usually inspired and assisted by customers.

- **Commitment to quality.** The process needs feedback loops at each stage to ensure quality assurance.

- **Relative state (to chief competitors) of technological development.** Innovation, to some extent, is self-fuelling: being ahead creates a pressure to stay ahead.

- **Fewer.** However they may do it, businesses need to focus resources on those innovations likely to perform best.

'Faster' measures:

- **Stretch time targets.** Whilst artificial deadlines tend to be counterproductive, a shared sense of immediacy can focus minds.

- **Frequency of meetings.** Many of us have a just-before-the-next-meeting approach to prioritization. The content or quality of the meeting matters less than the fact that it is happening.

- **Action-orientation.** Analysis paralysis exemplifies excellence as the enemy of the good. The modern trend is for 90% today rather than 99% next year but, again, that must depend on the nature of the innovation required.

'Cheaper' measures:

- **Thrift.** Poverty may not be the father of invention but imagination can be crippled by indulgence. The father of atomic research, Lord Rutherford, put it thus: 'We haven't the money, so we've got to think.'[1]

- **Recycling.** Using what exists rather than buying everything new. This also promotes learning from the past.

- **Benchmarking** competitors' costs.

Concerns with the metrics long list and alternatives

The boundary between culture and process is artificial. Provenance here determines how metrics are assigned to one or the other after eliminating duplications. The basis for actually measuring these 38 indicators, shown in Table C3 below, may not be obvious since some of them are really composites, e.g. 'sociability' is an index constructed from the answers to six questions. To trace the methodology for each one will distract us from the innovation health overview we are seeking. Closer examination of each tree does not help the view of the wood.

A general point should be registered about the fact that many of the measures can come only from internal staff surveys. That is also true of employee, or internal customer, corporate brand equity. Staff will tolerate filling in questionnaires only if they believe them to be worthwhile and if they are rare events. One can stretch frequency, in large companies, by careful sampling but these points remain:

- Innovation health and corporate brand equity surveys should normally be combined;

- Even if benchmarked with other companies, they remain subjective indicators of how staff care to report their perceptions, as distinct from objective measures.

An example of the latter problem, also from Chris Voss, is the 'excellence paradox'.[2] Top companies, as professionals, know the heights they have yet to achieve. As a result, they grade themselves modestly. At the other extreme, poor performers rate themselves as about average because they are unaware of world-class standards. Ignorance breeds complacency. The paradox then is that self-ratings may reflect the opposite of reality.

Does this invalidate self-assessment? Not really. It takes us back to the need to compare performance both with what firms are trying to achieve (plan) and with the market as a whole. Self-assessment will provide good answers to the former but not necessarily the latter. The two need to be separated explicitly by asking for assessments against what the firm's standards should be, and then again, against the standards elsewhere. Testing the respondents' knowledge of external comparisons, e.g. 'Did he/she work there?' determines the extent to which the external comparisons should be retained or ignored.

How positive the responses are may give a better impression of the overall helpfulness of the current culture than the individual answers. Nevertheless, surveys are a means of upward and downward communication that can be manipulated in ways that are little to do with metrics. For example, the recent idea that senior management bonuses should, in part, be tied to the outcomes of such surveys is nice but dumb. It is bound to distort the responses. More subtle, non-intrusive, measures should be used.

There is no complete answer to the inherent subjectivity of surveys for innovation health and corporate brand equity measurement but the odds can be improved by using outside professionals who can provide a broad database of comparable findings.

Additionally or alternatively, companies will look to non-survey sources. Most typically, internal matters of culture and process are ignored. Quantified outcomes can be compared with quantified innovation goals. Examples are provided by Table C1.

Table C1 ▪ Examples of goal-directed innovation metrics

Innovation goals	Initiatives	Innovation performance
Customer retention	New loyalty schemes	% customers lost
Increased new product innovation	No. of innovations launched	% successful paybacks/ shareholder value effects % of turnover due to products launched in last 3 years
Differential advantage	R&D expenditure Specific initiatives implemented	No. of patents registered
Market leadership	No. of new-to-the-world concepts initiated in period Type of market typically entered (new, mature, declining)	Average entry position (1st, 2nd ...) to market with new products and/or services

Discarded innovation health metrics

These few paragraphs record some objections to the other popular approaches encountered during our research. There is no suggestion the methods are wrong in principle or wrong for other purposes. They are addressed here only because, in moving towards a short list of innovation health metrics, their omission needs some justification.

The shareholder value approach forecasts the free cash flow from each proposed initiative, subtracts the cost of capital and chooses the highest discounted cash flow. Fine in theory but dubious in practice: no honest marketer can reliably do the arithmetic until some real market numbers show up. The arithmetic is still worth doing but only to remove some no-hopers.

A similar approach is to work back from share of revenue targets by estimating the expected success rate at each developmental stage from concept to mass market to derive the required number of new concepts per annum. That helps budgeting. Adequate resources are a necessary but insufficient condition. Conversely, excessive resources replace discipline with confusion. It is better to budget lean than fat as creative marketers are good poachers too. Resources aside, assessing innovations by their total number is plainly, in this environment of excess, counterproductive.

The most popular innovation metric in marketing is the share of revenue (or profit) represented by products launched within the last three, or five, years. This gives direction to the new product team and probably influences the approach to other marketing innovation too. The two difficulties are that measurement takes place a long time after the event and the figures can be manipulated with trivial variations.

Table C2 summarizes discarded metrics:

Table C2 ■ Discarded innovation health metrics

Metric	Reasons for elimination
Shareholder value	Not enough evidence for reliable forecasts but a helpful diagnostic for spotting no-hopers
Desired future share of revenue	Similar difficulties. More of a wish list than practical action
Share of current revenue/ profit from recent innovations	Popular and useful but with lagging indicators
Total number of innovations	Encourages quantity over quality, which is the opposite of most firms' needs
Number of innovations at each stage of the development process 'milestones passed'	A useful diagnostic to see the *flow* but not a metric of overall health

Long list of innovation health metrics

This section gathers together a long list of metrics following the model in Figure 6.1. Table C3 highlights those that seem most salient for most firms. It may seem that 38 are too many but they are a condensation of the wisdom from past research on innovation. Most of them have to be obtained from internal surveys and are accordingly subjective. This list was used as the base for refinement to the short list presented in Chapter 6.

Table C3 ■ Generic innovation health metrics

	Metrics
Leadership	1 Staff awareness of vision/direction
	2 Staff commitment to vision/direction
	3 Level of anxiety about the state of the business
	4 Trust in the leadership, e.g. perceived competence
	5 Leadership by example, e.g. risk taking, quality
	6 Active support by the leadership
	7 Perceived control (may be the reverse of autonomy below)
	8 Focus (reverse of initiative diversity)
Goals	9 Specificity of innovation goals, e.g. quantified
	10 Awareness of innovation goals
	11 Commitment to innovation goals
Resource adequacy	12 Finance availability
	13 Time availability
	14 Staffing (a mix of clever, creative, financially aware, networkers and task-oriented people)
Culture impacts on creativity, development and implementation	15 Encouragement of creativity
	16 Autonomy/delegation
	17 Challenging work
	18 Fun place to work
	19 Workload pressure (may be reverse of organizational slack)
	20 Organizational impediments (seen as reciprocal of experimentation's being expected of all managers)
	21 Learning culture, e.g. to what extent are failures celebrated, evaluated and broadcast?
	22 Supplier/customer involvement in the firm's innovation, e.g. suggesting new products or problems for solution
	23 Sociability
	24 Solidarity
	25 Valence of culture for innovation (+ve /–ve)
	26 Culture style/leadership fit with sector needs
Process (better, faster, cheaper)	27 Formality of process
	28 Organizational shape
	29 Incentives
	30 Commitment to quality
	31 Relative state (to chief competitors) of technological development

Table C3 ■ *Continued*

Metrics
32 Fewer (rapid elimination of improbables)
33 Stretch time targets
34 Frequency of meetings
35 Action-orientation
36 Thrift
37 Recycling
38 Benchmarking competitors' costs

References

1 According to Professor R.V. Jones in his Brunel Lecture, 14 February 1962.

2 Voss, Chris; Blackman, Kate; Hanson, Philip and Oak, Bryan (1995) 'The competitiveness of European manufacturing: a four country study', *Business Strategy Review* 6 (1: spring), 1–25.

Index

3M 51, 97, 99, 104-105, 107

AA (Automobile Association) 85
Aaker, Professor David 43
Abbey National 30–31
ACNeilsen 69, 135–136
Advertising and campaigns 154–155
  Assessment of 155–157
    Marketing expenditure 160–161
    Payment by results (PBR) 158
    System checklist 159–160
Agarwal, Professor Manoj K 63
Amabile, Professor Teresa 103–104, 105
Andersen Consulting 64–65
Assessment of marketing performance 6–7, 17–19
  Criteria for success 27–31
    Abbey National 30–31
    Bradford and Bingley 28–29
  Good planning practices 37–38
  Marketing in practice 19–25
    BAE Systems 23
    Bass Brewing 24–25, 26
    British Airways 20–21
    Cash flows 21
  Multiple brands 31–33
  Overview 17

Poor planning practices 37
Sector issues 33–35
System improvements 36
System test questionnaire 19
  Scores 39–40
Task force 35–36
Top-down 25–27
  Establishing goals 25
see also Performance assessment, process of
AT Kearney 35, 92
Automobile Association (AA) 85
Availability 67–68, 122–123
  see also Metrics
AXA Sun Life 85

BAE Systems 23
Balanced Scorecard 24, 26, 35, 102, 141, 148–149
Bass Brewing 24–25, 26
BAV (BrandAsset Valuator) 49
BBC 44
Benchmarking 29–30
Blyth, Lord 79
BMS (brand market segment) 90–91
BMU (brand market unit) 32–33
Bonner, Joseph 103–104
Bonuses, using metrics for 148–149

Boots the Chemist 9, 79–80
BP 123–125
BP Amoco 113
Bradford and Bingley 28–29
Brand, definition 4–5
Brand equity 41–46
    Availability 67–68
    BBC 44
    Commitment 66
    Consumer satisfaction 65–66
    Definition 5
    Evaluating brands 46–49
    Influence of 45
    Measurement, current approaches
        49–52
        3M 51
        Growth of 51
        Regularity of 52
        WPP BrandDynamics Pyramid
            49–50
        Y&R's BrandAsset Valuator 50
    Measurement, recommended
        approach 53–55
        Consumer brand equity overview
            53
    Metrics 14
    Monitoring changes 64–69
        Measuring metrics 68
    Overview 42
    Relative perceived quality 67
    Relative price 67
    Responsibility allocation 45
Brand Genetics 98
Brand market segment (BMS) 90–91
Brand market unit (BMU) 32–33
Brand valuation 46–49
    see also Brand equity
BrandAsset Valuator (BAV) 49
British Aerospace see BAE Systems
British Airways 20–21
British Gas see Centrica

Budgetary marketing, definition 4

Cadbury 7, 84
Cahalan, Nuala 71
Campaigns see Advertising and
    campaigns
Caradon plc 30
Carsberg, Sir Bryan 47, 141
CBI (Confederation of British
    Industry) 3
Centrica 81–82, 85
Chartered Institute of Marketing 28,
    29–30, 70
Chay, Richard 48
Commitment 66–67, 122–123
    see also Metrics
Confederation of British Industry
    (CBI) 3
Consumer satisfaction 65–66
    see also Metrics
Cutbill, Michael 71

Data gathering see Information
    organisation; Supplying metrics
Davidson, Hugh 80
DCF (discounted cash flow) 47
Dell, Michael 105
Delphi technique 74
Derivatives, definition 5–6
Diageo 32, 87
Diagnostics, definition 5
Discounted cash flow (DCF) 47
Double derivatives, definition 6
Duracell 86

Ehrenberg, Professor Andrew 42
EMAP 3, 91
Employee metrics 10, 15
    see also Metrics
Employer brand equity see Internal
    marketing metrics

Even More Offensive Marketing 80

FDS Market Research International
    138
Feldwick, Paul 42
Ferrari sponsorship 73–74
Financial metrics 63–64
  see also Metrics
Fitzgerald, Lin 147
Fluke Corporation 106
Forte 120
Freemans 71
Functional marketing, definition 4

Gallaher 10, 59
Geletkanycz, Professor Marta 70
Ghoshal, Professor Sumantra 24
Gillette 86
Granada 120
GrandMet 106

Hall and Partners 50–51
Hambrick, Professor Donald 70
Hamel, Gary 101
Heath, Robert 135
Hewtson Le Roux, Tim 51
Hippel, Eric von 104–105
Hooper, John 6, 11

IBM 62
ICAEW *see* Institute of Chartered
    Accountants of England and
    Wales
Incorporated Society of British
    Advertisers 6
Information organisation 11
Innovation 9–10, 95–98, 166–172
  Agenda items 108–110
  Culture 103–107
    Conceptual model 104, 105
    Dell 105

Fluke Corporation 106
Discarded metrics 170
Drivers/enablers/moderators 98–100
    Arthur D Little framework 100
  Key components 99
Goal-directed metrics 169
Metrics 15, 96, 110–111, 171–172
Process 107–108
  Novartis 107–108
Strategy 100–103
Institute of Chartered Accountants of
    England and Wales (ICAEW)
    141–142, 148
Institute of Work Psychology 118–119
Interbrand Newell Sorrell 46
Internal marketing metrics 113–114
  Business units 127–129
  Employee effect on company
    performance 118–121
    Nortel Networks 119
  Employee 'buy-in' 115–118
    Categories of employee 117
    Indicators of buy-in 116
  Multi-brand situation 125–127
    Employee metrics 127
  Unitary brand/business unit situation
    121–125
    BP 123–125
    Employer brand metrics 123
    TNT 122
  see also Metrics
International Accounting Standards
    Committee 47
International Distillers and Vintners
    Ltd 125

J&B Rare 60
JA Sharwood & Co 10, 101–102

Kaplan, Robert 24
  see also Balanced Scorecard

Kearon, John 98
Keller, Professor Kevin Lane 44

Lane Keller, Professor Kevin 44
Le Roux, Tim Hewtson 51
Lebas, Michel 152
Lloyds/TSB 7, 90
London Business School 28, 70, 141

Management incentives, using metrics
    for 149
Market and Opinion Research
    International see MORI
Market-based assets *see* Brand equity
Market Research News 138
Marketing, definition 3–4
Marketing & Communications Agency
    (MCA) 115–117
Marketing budget 160–161
Marketing metrics, list of 163–165
  see also Metrics
Marketing performance *see* Assessment
    of marketing performance;
    Performance
assessment, process of
Marketing Science Institute 34, 43–44
Marketing Society 81
Mars 30
Martins, Joe 106
MCA (Marketing & Communications
    Agency) 115–117
McDonald's 7, 70–71
McMahon, Sarah 64–65
Metrics 5
  Action recommendations 11–13
  Alignment/misalignment 150–152
    Future scenarios 151
  Brand equity 14
  Changing presentation 149–150
  Choosing 57–59
    Comparing methods 73–75

Ferrari sponsorship 73–74
  Shell 73–74
Defining the market segment
    59–61
Gallaher 59
General approach 61–69
  Andersen Consulting 64–65
  IBM 62
  Measuring metrics 68
  Profit and loss metrics 63
  Tailored approach 69–73
Employee 10, 15
Future use 147
Innovation 15
Key categories 7–9, 165
Marketing, list of 163–165
Misusing 147–149
Most commonly used 8
Profit and loss 14
see also Employee metrics; Internal
    marketing metrics; Supplying
    metrics
Meyer, Professor Marshall 86
Monsanto 72
MORI (Market & Opinion Research
    International) survey
    115–117

National Health Service 146
Nestlé 30, 83, 87, 91
Nortel Networks 119
Northridge, Nigel 59
Norton, David 24
  see also Balanced Scorecard
Novaction 88–89
Novartis 107–108

Pan-company marketing, definition
    3–4, 19–20
  Bass Brewery 24–25
  Marketing specialists 27

Payne, Professor Adrian 119
Pepsico 5
Performance assessment, process of
    77–78
  Board meetings 89–90
    Lloyds/TSB 90
  Segmentation and alignment 90–93
  Stages 78–80
    Boots the chemist 79–80
    Stage 1 80–82
      Centrica 81–82
      Investment priorities 81
    Stage 2 82–84
      Cadbury 84
      Nestlé 83
    Stage 3 85–86
      AA 85
      Duracell 86
    Stage 4 87–88
    Stage 5 88–89
   see also Assessment of marketing
     performance
Perrier, Raymond 46
Phoenix process 106
Pillsbury 32, 87
Procter & Gamble 6, 30, 83, 97, 107
Profit and loss metrics 14
  see also Metrics

Railtrack 147–148
Rao, Professor Vithala R 63
Relative perceived quality 67, 122–123
  see also Metrics
Relative price 67, 122–123
  see also Metrics
Relative satisfaction 122–123
Research agencies 135–139
Research International 50
Rolls Royce 34–35
Royal Mail 91

Sainsbury 30
Schneider, Ben 118
Sears 119–120
Shaw, Bob 46
Shell 30, 73–74, 134–135
Sheppard, Lord 6
Shocker, Professor Allan D 43–44
Sinclair, Bob 85
Skandia 86
Small/medium-sized enterprises see
    SMEs
SMEs (small/medium-sized
    enterprises) 26–27, 55, 88
Sonnack, Mary 103–104
Sony 32, 88
SPM (strategic performance measure)
    35, 91–93
Srivastava, Professor Rajendra K
    43–44
Strategic performance measurement
    (SPM) 35, 91–93
Sunderland, John 84
Supplying metrics 131–133
  Auditing needs 133–135
    Shell 134–135
  Data supply 135–139
  Packaging and presenting 140–144
    ICAEW recommended
     performance indicators 142
  Segment selection 139–140
  see also Metrics

Taylor Nelson Sofres 136
Tesco 52
TNT 122

Underwood, Elaine 101–102
Unilever 30, 83, 87

Valuation of brand 46–49
  see also Brand equity

value-based management (VBM) 79
VBM (value-based management) 79
von Hippel, Professor Eric 104–105
von Wartburg, Professor Walter
  107–108
Voss, Professor Chris 108, 166–168

Wartburg, Professor Walter von
  107–108

Water industry 147
Waugh, Simon 81
Willis, Steve 85
WPP 137
  BrandDynamics Pyramid model
    49–50

Young and Rubicam 49, 66
  BrandAsset Valuator 50